OXFORDSHIRE AT WAR

Oxford in wartime: soldiers and women undergraduates share the pavement in High Street near Queen's College.

OXFORDSHIRE AT WAR

MALCOLM GRAHAM

OXFORDSHIRE BOOKS

ALAN SUTTON PUBLISHING LIMITED

First published in the United Kingdom in 1994
Alan Sutton Publishing Limited
Phoenix Mill · Far Thrupp · Stroud · Gloucestershire

Oxfordshire Books · Oxfordshire County Council · Leisure and Arts
Central Library · Westgate · Oxford

First published in the United States of America in 1994
Alan Sutton Publishing Inc.
83 Washington Street · Dover · NH 03820

British Library Cataloguing in Publication Data

A catalogue record for this book is available from the British Library

ISBN 0-7509-0459-3

Library of Congress Cataloging in Publication Data applied for

Jacket illustrations, clockwise from top left: evacuees leaving Oxford station,
1939; woman welding at Morris Motors in Cowley, 1943; Spitfire 'City of
Oxford', 1940; soldiers and women undergraduates in Oxford High Street;
paying in the week's savings at Lewknor; tanks fitted with anti-aircraft guns at
Cowley, 1944.

Typeset in 11/12 Ehrhardt.
Typesetting and origination by
Alan Sutton Publishing Limited.
Printed in Great Britain by
Hartnolls, Bodmin, Cornwall.

Contents

Preface

This book covers the county of Oxfordshire as constituted in 1974, and includes towns and villages in the Vale of the White Horse which were part of the administrative county of Berkshire during the Second World War. General references to Oxfordshire derived from contemporary sources only apply to the historic county.

Imperial measures and pounds, shillings and pence have been retained throughout. These conversion tables are included for the benefit of readers who have grown up in a metric and decimal world:

Length

1 inch (in)		2.54 centimetres
1 foot (ft)	12 in	0.30 metre
1 yard (yd)	3 ft	0.91 metre
1 mile	1,760 yd	1.61 kilometres

Area

1 acre	4,840 sq yd	0.40 hectare

Capacity

1 pint		0.57 litre
1 gallon	8 pints	4.55 litres

Weight

1 ounce (oz)		28.35 grams
1 pound (lb)	16 oz	0.45 kilos
1 hundredweight (cwt)	112 lb	50.8 kilos
1 ton	20 cwt	1.02 tonnes

Money

1 penny (*d*)	½p
2*d*	1p
6*d*	2½p
1 shilling (*s*)	5p
2*s*	10p
5*s*	25p
10*s*	50p
£1	£1.00

Acknowledgements

Most of the illustrations in this book are taken from the Oxfordshire Photographic Archive, a major resource for the county's history, which is managed by Oxfordshire County Council's Department of Leisure and Arts. The Archive is based in the Centre for Oxfordshire Studies at Oxford Central Library (tel. 0865–815432) and welcomes public enquiries and offers the opportunity to borrow   and copy old photographs of the county.

I am indebted to the following people and institutions for permission to reproduce their photographs:

British Motor Industry Heritage Trust, jacket: top right, middle left; COD Bicester, p. 61; John Dossett-Davies, pp. 108, 166; Imperial War Museum, pp. 72, 77, 125, jacket: bottom left; Brian Lowe, pp. 120, 98, 100; The Brian Lowe/Peter Wright Collection, p. 96; Malvern College, p. 37; Brian Mobley, p. 171; Oxford City Council, pp. 90, 91, 129; Oxfordshire Archives, p. 26; Oxfordshire Health Authority, p. 14; *Punch*, pp. 34, 134; John Rawlins, p. 23; Angela Spencer-Harper, pp. 105, 126; Laurence Waters, p. 156; Tom Worley, pp. 131, 167.

An Oxford Mail *newsvendor hurries from Newspaper House after Neville Chamberlain's broadcast, carrying the special edition which announced that Britain was at war with Germany.*

CHAPTER ONE

The Outbreak of War

> I am speaking to you from the Cabinet Room at 10, Downing Street. This morning, the British Ambassador in Berlin handed the German Government an official Note stating that unless we heard from them by 11 o'clock that they were prepared at once to withdraw their troops from Poland, a state of war would exist between us. I have to tell you that no such undertaking has been received, and that consequently this country is at war with Germany.[1]

The Prime Minister, Neville Chamberlain, broadcast this message and the end of his hopes for peace at 11.15 a.m. on Sunday 3 September 1939. Many people heard the momentous news on the wireless at home, and the fateful speech was relayed to churchgoers at the morning service in St Giles' Church, Oxford:

> As the solemn words of Mr Chamberlain echoed through the building there was a deep hush, and for a few moments after he had finished we sat there immoveable, until the voice of Canon Diggle, the vicar, was heard leading us in prayer.[2]

At St Mary's Church in Banbury, the vicar, Revd A.L.E. Williams, finished his sermon and

> read from the pulpit a note which had been handed to him while he was addressing the congregation, and briefly announced that Britain was now in a state of war with Germany, as the Prime Minister's message had just come through to the Nation and the Empire.[3]

The international crisis had prevented the Mounthill Rambling Club from going on their planned outing to the Sussex Downs, and the Kennington group travelled instead to Burford, arriving at about 11 a.m.:

> The main street of Burford was full of women and children, apparently evacuated from London, and when we stopped to look for a place to obtain coffee, we felt the eyes of people upon us who appeared to be puzzled, and curious to know what we were doing on such a serious occasion. We made our way to a small café owned by Mrs Nash, High St, Burford. . . . It was while we were drinking our coffee that Mr Chamberlain Broadcast to the Nation at 11.15 a.m., and informed us that no reply had been received to the Government's Note to Hitler, and we were therefore now at War with Germany.

The Burford café where members of the Mounthill Rambling Club heard that war had been declared.

The news was received with silence. There was no mad cheering, no mass hysteria, but everyone seemed to realize the seriousness of the Government's decision.

Outside in the main street of Burford we could see the sun shining, while inside a canary sang merrily in a cage. . . . Mrs Nash was nearly in tears and informed me that she had two sons both of military age.[4]

Others learned of the outbreak of war from a hurriedly prepared special edition of the *Oxford Mail*:

Crowds on Carfax and in the centre of Oxford eagerly bought copies of the 'Oxford Mail' from the newspaper sellers as they heard them shout that war was declared. Motorists stopped their cars to buy papers, and the people stood around in little groups reading the news. There was a general expression of relief that the period of uncertainty had ended.

By the early afternoon, copies of the paper were on sale in Banbury and, again, a feeling of relief was detected.[5] Other people were less sanguine and Brian Mobley, then a young man in Oxford, recalled how he felt when war was declared:

I think a sense of stepping into the unknown and yet it wasn't really because we had seen what had happened in Spain and we had seen what had happened in Poland. No, I think excitement wrapped up with fear. I think everybody, especially us younger ones who were all, being of the age we were, wrapped up in aeroplanes, could see what the Luftwaffe was and the power they'd got and what they had done and I think we all expected they would be here tomorrow after the day war was declared and thrash everything into the ground.[6]

The Mounthill Ramblers decided to continue their Cotswold walk through Taynton and Great Rissington to Bourton-on-the-Water,[7] but, across the county, a new urgency was injected into preparations for war. At Chipping Norton all the emergency services were called out at once and the St John Ambulance Brigade and the fire brigade stood by at their headquarters in case of air attacks. The *Oxford Mail*'s special edition addressed a warning comprising sixteen points about air-raid precautions to 'The General Public of Oxford', and in Banbury work continued throughout the day to try to complete the public air-raid shelters.[8] In Bicester that evening 'air-raid wardens and special constables toured the streets and gave warning where lights were showing'.[9] Evacuees, both official and unofficial, continued to pour into the county and an unexpected party of about 800 mothers and young children arrived at Banbury station at about 6 p.m. A further 1,800 evacuees were brought by train to Oxford on 3 September and, on arrival, had cause to thank the women of Cripley Road, the so-called 'angels' of West Oxford, who

provide seating accommodation on the pavements outside their homes, and as soon as a contingent of evacuees arrives they serve them with cups of tea, water, and anything else which may be wanted.[10]

A tea break at Bourton-on-the-Water for the Mounthill Ramblers, who decided not to let war curtail their Cotswold outing on 3 September.

Places of public entertainment were immediately closed and, despite glorious sunshine, local people, evacuees and Territorials alike were unable to take advantage of Banbury Corporation swimming pool.[11] In Wallingford the closure of the Regal Cinema left evacuees with nothing to do, but parents who made the journey from London that day were said to be delighted with the place and the arrangements that had been made for the welfare of their children.[12]

There were no local air-raid warnings on 3 September but, as darkness fell and the black-out was enforced with a new rigour, many people must have wondered what the next day would bring. It was a time of great anxiety relieved by courage and determination. A London boy who had been evacuated to Witney wrote to his parents later that week:

Dear Pop and Mum,
I hope you are quite safe. And I heard the air raid waning on Wnesday, I hope you are well because I am safe. I hope you are not worring about the war we are going to win the war. We are quite happy. When I heard the air raid waning I never move so quick in all my life. good day from Ronald.[13]

The *Bicester Advertiser* carried the message:

KEEP A GOOD HEART. WE ARE GOING TO WIN THROUGH.[14]

Children in Windmill Road, Oxford, watch with interest as City Council workmen construct a public air-raid shelter in early September 1939.

CHAPTER TWO

Air-raid Precautions

Fear of devastating air raids including the probability of gas attacks led to a strong emphasis on ARP as the international situation deteriorated in the mid-1930s. Oxfordshire County Council received a report suggesting ways of dividing the county up for Civil Defence purposes as early as May 1936[1], but the Air Raid Precautions Act of 1937 provided for the establishment of a service operated locally by county and county borough councils under the overall direction of central government.

In the next two years the ARP service was brought into being and started to prepare for the worst. Oxford City Council set up an ARP Committee in 1938 and, in the aftermath of the Munich crisis, an exhibition was held in the Town Hall in December to show people how to protect themselves and their homes in

The city's ARP Control Centre in the basement of Oxford Town Hall, illustrated in February 1942. Reports from wardens' posts throughout the city were received in this room and plotted on the wall chart.

the event of air raids. In April 1939 the Chief Constable, C.R. Fox, was appointed ARP Controller for the city[2] and Oxford was divided into 11 areas which were further subdivided into 210 sectors with 1,337 volunteer wardens and 70 wardens' posts. A control centre was established underneath the Town Hall, first aid posts were set up and two ambulance depots were provided, one in Norham Mews and the other in Cowley Place; the latter was chosen because it could serve the eastern half of Oxford if Magdalen Bridge was bombed. Five auxiliary fire stations were in readiness and thirty light trailer pump teams were available to put out minor fires. Rescue parties had been identified from among the city's building firms and Council employees were trained to act as gas decontamination squads. Most ominously perhaps, 95,000 gas masks had been distributed and decontamination stations had been set up where victims of gas attacks could have a shower bath and eye treatment and be 'lent sufficient clothing to enable them to go to their homes in decency after treatment'.[3]

Oxfordshire County Council appointed Major F.G. Scott as County ARP Controller, and in May 1938 the county was divided into six sub-areas centred on Banbury, Bicester, Chipping Norton, Henley, Wheatley and Witney. Each sub-area appointed its own committee to establish stores for the necessary supplies, identify suitable premises for the various elements of the service and consider the provision of public air-raid shelters.[4] By June 1939 Wantage had two wardens' posts, one at St Katherine's and the other at the Town Hall; in the event of air raids, three first aid parties, a decontamination squad and a demolition and rescue party would be ready to serve the town and surrounding villages.[5] ARP seemed just as vital in a small village like Benson:

> To start with of course, we, like most people in England assumed that we should be bombed incessantly, especially as we were so near to an Aerodrome. Shelters were built by the authorities for many of the more exposed cottages, and some by private people. . . . Not only did we expect bombing, but we also expected to be attacked by gas, so very early we began preparing gas shelters and the Wardens were busy fitting gas masks. . . .[6]

Even in apparently safer places such as the Bartons, volunteers were quick to create a service which comprised 10 wardens, 8 first aiders, 3 messengers, an ambulance driver and an ambulance attendant.[7]

As war became increasingly likely during August 1939, preparations took on a new urgency. Abingdon claimed to be the first town in England to reach its official quota of wardens, and at the outbreak of war was said to be 'ready for any eventuality'.[8] Oxford, too, was said to be ready for the worst with special constables controlling the city's air-raid sirens and workmen blacking out the white reflecting surfaces of the traffic islands in St Giles'. At the Bodleian, the library's most valuable items were moved into the basement of the New Bodleian Library, to be followed by pictures from Christ Church, stained glass from New College and manuscripts from Merton and Balliol; these treasures were joined by the King's Library from the British Museum, the Dyce Collection from the Victoria and Albert Museum and by books and specimens from the herbarium at Kew Gardens. At the same time, the Ashmolean Museum packed works of art for safe storage in the country and workmen boarded up the stained glass windows in All Souls' College chapel.[9] On 1 September Oxford had its first taste of black-out

An optimistic advertisement by Knowles & Son, the Oxford building firm, published during the 'Phoney War'. It was quickly replaced by a warning to be ready for bombs after the success of the German blitzkrieg in May 1940.

conditions as street-lighting was reduced to just 153 lamps along main roads; in the gloom, motorists criticized cyclists riding without lights, special constables argued with drivers who refused to do without their headlights and groups of pedestrians were accused of walking arm-in-arm in the centre of the road.[10]

With the Prime Minister's statement on Sunday 3 September that the country was now at war with Germany, it seemed only a matter of time before the ARP services were tested in earnest. Didcot had its first warning at 7.40 a.m. on 6 September:

There was no alarm, and, in fact, the difficulty was to keep people off the streets. It appeared that as officers cycled around blowing their whistles and warning the population to take cover, more and more came out to their front gates to satisfy their curiosity.[11]

In Bicester most townsfolk stayed indoors during the same alert, but

Workers . . . continued on their way to their places of employment, Urban Council employees could be seen calmly proceeding with their task in the streets, and one milkman whistled merrily as he continued his round.[12]

If the patience of local air-raid wardens was tested by this cavalier disregard of their warnings, they were at least spared the humiliation of one warden in Oxford who commandeered a bike and set off to shepherd people back into their homes:

All goes well until he reaches one street, which is a slight slope. Puffing manfully upward, in all the glory of his equipment (he couldn't manage the rattle or the bell as both his hands were occupied in steering the cycle, and he couldn't manage the whistle because he wanted all his breath) the warden evoked a cheer from those daring citizens strolling in the open. Spotting a group of these idlers engaged in gossip he put on an extra spurt to get to them and disperse them quickly, when disaster overtook him – his helmet fell off into the road with a loud clang! Loud and ribald laughter greeted this unfortunate contretemps, and one of the onlookers was heard to remark, 'Coo, now the poor little blighter's hat's fallen off!'[13]

A policeman wearing his gas mask and a sandwich-board man advertising black-out materials promote the message of ARP in Queen Street, Oxford, in 1939.

The long-suffering warden was, however, able to take comfort from the rigorous enforcement of the black-out regulations, and the stentorian cry 'Put that light out' soon became all too familiar. Minty's in Oxford advertised the availability of black-out material and Pankhurst's in Bicester hurriedly acquired 'Strong Black Paper' in 36 in, 60 in and 90 in widths 'Specially Manufactured for Window Blanking'.[14] Less conventional material was used at Post L111 in New Marston where a soaked warden arrived to find that the legs of his spare pair of trousers had been amputated for use as black-out curtains.[15] The Courts soon began to fill up with black-out offenders and, in September 1939, a Banbury man was fined £1 for failing to obscure a bedroom light and compounding the offence by using abusive language to the policeman who informed him about it; on the other hand, a farmworker at Balscote was let off after making the doubtful excuse, 'I was just going to put something up at the window, when the constable knocked at the door'.[16]

The black-out affected many aspects of everyday life, depriving people of lighted telephone boxes and public clocks and forcing churches to change the times of their services; in December it was even said to be encouraging demand for a strain of white alsatians which could be seen in the dark.[17] All workplaces had to be completely screened and it took five days to black-out the windows of Oxford Town Hall.[18] If all this was inconvenient, the black-out became extremely dangerous on the roads where drivers had to feel their way along unlit streets with only a little help from masked headlights. The number of accidents rose sharply and, in the early weeks of the war, County Council employees were active in Bicester whitening the pavement edges and painting white lines to assist the movement of traffic.[19] In Oxford H.W.B. Joseph, a Fellow of New College and member of the City's Evacuation Committee, noted in his diary:

> Much money is being spent on white paint. First a broken central white line was placed down the centre of all principal roads; then the curbs were painted at corners, and before lamp-posts; then on principal roads on the whole length; now bands of white are being painted round trees in St Giles's, lamp-posts, &c.[20]

A speed limit of 20 m.p.h. was introduced in February 1940, although a man fined for travelling at 30 m.p.h. in St Giles' could argue with some justification that he had been unable to 'see his speedometer because his dashboard was not illuminated'.[21] On the pavements, Oxford tried to solve the problem of people blundering into each other in the dark by affixing red signs warning PEDESTRIANS PLEASE KEEP LEFT to city centre lamp-posts.[22] In rural areas the black-out was total and, around Benson, 'there was a complete absence of farm and cottage lights twinkling around the countryside'.[23] Enforcement in Oxford proved more difficult and, in November, there were complaints about poorly screened colleges and thoughtless maids who drew blinds early in the morning and then switched on the lights to tidy grates and get on with their household duties.[24] More seriously, aerial observation in January 1940 showed that the black-out above Oxford was largely nullified by car headlights and by traffic lights which could be seen changing from a height of 2,000 ft.[25] Nevertheless, to a visiting American, J.F. Fulton,

Oxford on a full moonlit night with all artificial illumination suppressed, presents a sight that is utterly unforgettable. The lights and shadows and glorious silhouettes of buildings against the autumn sky are sights that few have beheld . . . and the thought of any injury befalling these landmarks is so disturbing that one banishes it completely from thought.[26]

To the economy-minded the enforced darkness worked wonders for the street-lighting budget and, in December 1939, the *Chipping Norton Advertiser* trumpeted the news, 'Black-out is saving Banbury over £1,000 a year'.[27]

Against daylight attacks the art of camouflage was used to disguise strategic targets. At the Cowley works the outside walls and even the chimneys were coated with a sickly green paint in an attempt to break up the shape of these large and distinctive structures.[28] A dummy aluminium factory was built 3 miles north of Banbury to distract attention from the Northern Aluminium Company's premises.[29] The White Horse near Uffington was retired beneath a covering of turf for the duration of the war, and the same fate befell a prominent vehicle turning circle at Beacon Hill reservoir.[30] The camouflage at the De Havilland plant at Witney, designed by Hugh Casson, was so effective that pilots had difficulty finding the aerodrome![31] At Swinford waterworks Oxford City Council battled with eventual success against the Ministry of Home Security's plan 'to paint over the exteriors of the buildings and the boundary walls. This would have meant irreparable damage to the fine appearance of the works.'[32]

In larger urban areas air-raid shelters had been identified in existing buildings, but purpose-built structures were now urgently needed and places with no communal facilities began to agitate for them. At the outbreak of war, Banbury

Static water tank in Faringdon Market Place in 1945. If the mains supply had been disrupted by air-raid damage, fire-fighters would have relied on these alternative sources of water.

had accommodation for 750 people in shelters situated in Hunt, Edmunds malt house cellars in Bridge Street, the Town Hall, the Gas Company offices and Broughton and Wilkes' cellars in the Market Place.[33] In central Oxford refuge was to be found in a wide variety of buildings including Balliol College and Christ Church, the Grapes in George Street, the crypt of St Peter in the East Church and cellars beneath the Covered Market. Street shelters were still being built in suburban Oxford in September 1939 and nine more were hurriedly completed in Abingdon, although the Borough Council was soon complaining that they had no roofs.[34] In Witney slit trenches provided some shelter among the trees on Church Green.[35] Even in the summer of 1940, however, Faringdon was still without a public shelter because Berkshire County Council preferred to provide free materials for private shelters. An editorial in the *Faringdon Advertiser* urged the Tradesmen's Association to act to protect local shoppers because the loss of life from an air raid would be 'a dreadful blot on the town. . . . Faringdon would be boycotted by shoppers from the villages for many a long day.' The town's problem was at last resolved in August when T.H. Tayler of the Crown Hotel made his cellars available.[36]

If shelters and the signs pointing to them became a prominent feature in wartime towns so too did the preparations for fire-fighting. In Oxford 4 in pipes were laid along the gutters of principal streets and static water tanks were built to provide emergency water supplies. The city's largest water tank was in Between Towns Road, but there was another large one in Radcliffe Square and Merton College erected a tank of its own 'constructed so as to harmonise with the surroundings'.[37]

While air-raid precautions gathered momentum outside, a host of booklets, newspaper advertisements and even cigarette cards urged householders to 'Make Your Home Safe Now'. A safe refuge was to be found, preferably in a cellar or

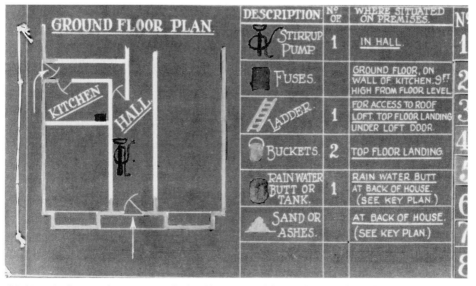

Making the home safe; one page of a booklet produced by the householders of Nos 1–8 Linton Road, Oxford, to indicate the whereabouts of equipment for extinguishing incendiary bombs.

basement, and this could be made gas-proof by sealing cracks, windows and fireplaces and by fixing a carpet or blanket over the door. Windows could be protected with sandbags, wire netting, transparent wrapping material, mosquito netting, stout paper or heaps of books. These refuges could then be equipped with food, drink, clothing, some means of entertainment, fire-fighting equipment and other useful items.[38] At one Oxford college arrangements displayed a worrying lack of foresight:

> The shelter, a converted cellar, has only one entrance. Instructions which have been issued point out that if a bomb falls nearby and makes escape by this one door impossible, the inhabitants can dig themselves out with a pick-axe which has been provided for the purpose! Then it is announced that this useful tool will be kept in the porter's lodge – at least 200 yards away. Apparently the non-arrival of the dons for dinner will be the signal for the excavation to begin.[39]

Sand dumps were established in Thame and residents were asked to take a large bucketful per house and store it conveniently for use against incendiary bombs.[40] In Oxford householders took too literally an instruction to keep water in the bath at night and had to be advised that a few bucketfuls would suffice.[41] With the help of a stirrup pump they were then equipped to extinguish incendiary bombs in the home and transfer them to a Redhill container, a specially designed bucket filled with sand, by using a long-handled scoop and hoe. As the threat of raids increased in 1940, hundreds of Oxford people attended stirrup pump demonstrations given by Inspector Miller of the City Police.[42] Houses with these pumps were issued with enamelled notices drawing attention to the fact and residents in Linton Road in North Oxford prepared a booklet illustrating the whereabouts of fire-fighting equipment.[43]

Later in the war, Oxford as a vulnerable area was issued with Anderson shelters which held four or more people and were generally erected in back gardens. They were made of corrugated steel sheets which were sunk into the ground, bolted together and covered with earth so that the occupants were only at risk from a direct hit. The indoor Morrison shelter, a mesh steel cage with a steel top that could be used as a table, was also made available by Oxford City Council in May 1942, but few were issued locally.[44] One recipient wrote despairingly to the Town Clerk:

> Dear Sir
> We have tryed to Elect our shelter but cannot, for sides says tops, don't know which from which. My son home on leave now going back Wednesday tryed also. All we succeeded in was smashing the glass to pieces out of an hero's photo. May some one show us please.[45]

Even with the Morrison shelter erected it could only be of use if it was occupied during an air raid. This was not always the case in one Oxford house:

> Mother had given us older children strict instructions, should the siren go in the middle of the night we were to grab our clothes and as many babies as possible, then downstairs and into the shelter. One night, the siren went, mother woke us up, and the rush downstairs followed. Into the shelter went the

Cowley children, watched by anxious parents, have their gas masks fitted in 1939.

young ones, my mother, and myself, but not my two brothers. Although two years between their ages, at that time they were the same size, and that very day had each been bought new boots, also the same size. Now one had got the other's boots on. WAR!!! That had nothing on those two. They fought, argued and squabbled, and when they eventually sorted things out we could hear the tail end of the 'all clear'.[46]

Fear of gas attacks formed the other vital impetus for ARP work. Gas masks for older children and adults had been issued before the war and, in early September 1939, Banbury people were warned:

Persons over 4½ years old should examine their respirators, see that they are undamaged and satisfy themselves that they can put them into use speedily if required.[47]

Gas masks for babies and younger children were available in Oxford in early 1940 and reached Banbury and Faringdon by March. Wardens in Faringdon arranged, perhaps wisely, that

only those over two years of age could be brought to be fitted, instructions being given to the mothers by means of a life-sized doll in the case of the babies' helmets. It was a happy idea on the part of someone to have them made in colours for the kiddies, and, of course, to put a thing on with a tongue hanging out, appeals to the shy ones and also the mischievous.[48]

Some children did in fact develop quite an affection for these Mickey Mouse respirators and were reluctant to part with them. In 1943 Bicester parents had to be warned that these masks were useless once children had outgrown them.[49] In the early months of the war gas detector boards were put up in various parts of Bicester and, in Oxford, people's curiosity must have been excited by this notice:

> City of Oxford Air Raid Precautions
> GAS DETECTION
> The Top of this Pillar Box has
> been specially treated for the
> detection of gas. IT MUST NOT
> BE TOUCHED OR INTERFERED
> WITH IN ANY WAY
>   CITY ENGINEER, OXFORD[50]

At first, people carried their gas masks everywhere and the Northern Aluminium Company in Banbury threatened not to admit employees who arrived without them.[51] Wearing the thing to work was a different matter as Oxford warden D43 discovered when he was ridiculed for doing so in the autumn of 1940.[52]

Surgeons at Oxford's Churchill Hospital on gas mask drill early in 1942.

Having volunteered for a task which proved hectic, unpopular and potentially dangerous, this head warden in Oxford was probably expressing feelings that many colleagues would have shared:

> I'm just a poor Head Warden,
> Once without a care,
> But now, upon this service,
> My head is bowed and bare.
>
> My wife has turned against me;
> One can't blame her a bit.
> She says that now I'm always
> Busy sorting kit.
>
> The 'phone is always ringing,
> Its buzz has never ceased,
> Since Posts were ordered to be manned,
> And staffs to be increased.
>
> It's either 'Can I have a mask?'
> Or 'Can I have a rattle?'
> Then, 'What about my helmet, sir—'
> And so they like to prattle!
>
> 'Please, sir, this post ain't no damned good,
> The draught is something awful,
> I've got cold feet already,
> It ain't quite right and lawful.'
>
> 'What about my baby, sir?'
> A female voice comes through.
> 'If I don't get my bag at once
> There'll be no peace for you.'
>
> Post Double-X is short of bells,
> Gas curtains, masks and kit,
> And Warden So-and-So's resigned
> Because his boots don't fit.
>
> Then, Big Chief telephones to say
> Would I mind getting busy,
> For Mrs Blank (I know her well!)
> Needs small-size mask for Lizzie.
>
> The day wears on, and wearily
> I settle down to slumber,
> When Office ARP rings up
> To give a new Post number.
>
> Then into bed at last I get,
> A giddy, nervous wreck,
> Torn and troubled with a dream
> of ARP – OH HECK![53]

The Chipping Norton gas decontamination squad in action. This photograph may have been taken in December 1939 during a mock gas bomb attack.

During the first months of the war many exercises were held to improve the efficiency of the ARP service. In the Wallingford area, for instance, an exercise was held on 8 October 1939 which resulted in 'only a few minor mistakes that could easily be rectified'.[54] Abingdon and Oxford held large-scale practices on 10 December and, a week later, Oxfordshire staged a massive event in all six areas with an imaginary air raid, a plane crash at Sandford-on-Thames and a mustard gas attack on Chipping Norton.[55] At the same time schools and factories were also concerned to perfect their reactions to air raids. On 17 May 1940 Winifred Bennett, the headmistress of Albury and Tiddington school, reported:

> This afternoon we had a practice for air-raid precautions; and have decided that if anti-aircraft firing is heard we shall draw blinds in school and carry on, but if a siren is heard first we shall divide into two parties, one going to Tiddington House Cellar and the other to Mr W. Silver, Manor Farm, and into the cellar there. Each party of children will be in charge of a teacher. Time taken in the above – 4 minutes.[56]

In Oxford the University used 'spotters' to warn of danger from daylight raids, but was equally determined that work should proceed wherever possible:

> If there is a raid warning before an examination candidates will be expected to appear half-an-hour after the 'Raiders Passed' has been given. If a warning is given in the course of an examination, the paper will be immediately concluded and candidates will go to the nearest air-raid shelter.[57]

At Pressed Steel in Cowley every effort was made to provide the perfect ARP organization with a permanently manned control room, area wardens and about

400 volunteers, some of whom would be acting as look-outs on the factory roofs in the event of a raid.[58]

With the fall of France in May 1940 the effectiveness of all these preparations was soon to be tested by the first enemy attacks on local targets. Raids began in June, concentrating at first upon airfields such as Weston-on-the-Green which was attacked on eleven separate occasions between June 1940 and May 1941. Local civilians were little affected by such raids and, when ten bombs landed harmlessly in fields after apparently being targeted at the Otmoor Bombing Range, the County ARP Controller reported:

> the general state is one of calmness, and almost suggesting a satisfying amusement that the enemy should have wasted so many bombs by dropping them into open country.[59]

All this began to change in the autumn as first Banbury and then Witney came under attack. The raid on Banbury occurred on 3 October and a censored account of it was published in next week's *Banbury Guardian*:

RAID ON A MIDLAND TOWN

On a recent afternoon on a Midland town at which the market was in progress a sudden raid was made by a Dornier bomber, with some fatal results. People in the yard of the Cattle Market saw the bomber suddenly emerge from a cloud and swooping down, drop bombs in its immediate vicinity. None fell within the sale yard and the business proceeded. Several, however, fell in a yard adjacent and loss of life was occasioned. The ARP Services turned out with most

ARP Rescue squad at the Northern Aluminium Company's Banbury factory, c. 1940. Behind the group, a single-storey building displays wartime camouflage and protective shutters.

commendable promptitude, and . . . it was a striking demonstration of the efficiency of local services.[60]

Six people were killed in the attack and several were injured. Two of the town's three gasometers were destroyed, reducing the gas storage capacity by 82 per cent, several fires were started and the railway was damaged near Banbury South signal-box.[61]

Witney was hit by two bombs during the night of 21/2 November. Since most people were in bed there were no serious casualties, but 220 houses were damaged. The *Witney Gazette* was 'unable to publish the details when the news is hot' but, in the following week's issue, described the effects on a town in the Home Counties:

The Church had most of its windows blown in or damaged, the adjacent Hall, Police Station, Council Offices suffering equally badly through taking the full force of the blast. The nearby school will be unusable for several weeks. Another bomb exploded near some Council houses and cottages, necessitating the evacuation of some of the tenants. A range of buildings near by took the full

Repairing bomb damage in Witney after the town was hit by two bombs during the night of 21/2 November 1940.

force of the second bomb and was utterly destroyed. Many plate glass shop fronts were broken, but small panes suffered little damage. . . .[62]

The anxiety aroused by such incidents was further fuelled by the arrival of thousands of evacuees from the London Blitz and by the bombing of Coventry. To those in the south of the county the Blitz was so close that F.P. Chamberlain at Benson could see the anti-aircraft guns of London firing like sparks from a blacksmith's anvil.[63] The waves of bombers heading for Coventry were clearly audible over much of the county and E.J. Lainchbury of Kingham wrote in his journal:

November 14th, 1940. Thursday 8.30 p.m. For the last 1½ hours German bombers have been over us, apparently looking for Rissington aerodrome. . . .

November 17th, 1940. Sunday. My opening remark in the last entry that German bombers had been over us for 1½ hours did not give its entire significance, for then I did not know but now I do. For hours a constant stream of bombers was passing over us on its way to Coventry, which was bombed terribly. The Germans say 500 machines took part. The English say there were 1,000 casualties and the city has been devastated. Charles went up there the next morning and was not able to reach his destination owing to debris, unexploded bombs, fires, and all the rest.[64]

In Banbury there were persistent rumours that one of Lord Haw-Haw's sinister broadcasts from Germany had included the warning that 'our bombers will deal with Banbury' now that Birmingham and Coventry had been bombed.[65] The Northern Aluminium Company produced a special ARP edition of its journal in November 1940, informing employees that the old advice that they would receive at least eight minutes' warning of a raid no longer applied:

The course of recent events has altered this completely, and has necessitated our being in a position *to take shelter within a matter of seconds*.[66]

In these circumstances men of the Royal Observer Corps were constantly scanning the skies from posts at Stadhampton, Watlington Hill and Shipton-under-Wychwood[67] while volunteers watched anxiously in their localities. At Benson, for instance, local women formed a rota to watch from the church tower for an hour either side of sunrise and sunset; if they saw anything, they were to drop a message to a runner stationed at the bottom who would rush it to the police.[68]

In Oxford at the beginning of 1941, householders in Northmoor Road between Linton Road and Belbroughton Road organized their own firewatching rota.[69] Anticipating a renewed German onslaught in the spring of 1941, the Government made firewatching compulsory in February and central Oxford businesses formed a Fire Fighters' and Watchers' Corps which was divided into seven sub-areas under Area Commandant E.J. Day. Watch towers were set up, for example, at All Saints' Church and on Woolworth's roof, and Mr Roper described arrangements in sub-area 1 on 28 February:

'R' Block at the Morris Motors Cowley factory, c. 1942, showing the ingenious camouflage which was intended to confuse enemy pilots. In the foreground, employees are putting the finishing touches to three Tiger Moths.

There was a joint scheme between Lloyds Bank and Sainsburys. Three persons on duty each night. In case of danger the watch would be doubled. Four persons one male and three female on duty all day Sunday in two hour shifts. Thursday afternoon was covered by Lloyds. The International Stores have two paid Fire Watchers. International and Ross Café have no equipment. Lennards and Margetts getting their equipment now. Mowbrays have necessary equipment and one person was sleeping at Kings.[70]

Both city and county, however, continued to escape the horrors of heavy bombing and suffered only isolated incidents. On 22 March 1941 twenty bombs were dropped along a line from the Wildsmoor Estate to RAF Abingdon, damaging eleven houses and causing one serious injury. The attack also cut one of Oxford Waterworks' service pipes, inflicting the only wartime damage to a system that had prepared for the worst by acquiring mobile pumps to take water straight from the Thames and installing twenty emergency drinking-water tanks in and around Oxford.[71] On 9 April a bomb exploded in a street between Littlemore and Cowley causing a boulder to crash through the roof of a house and on to an empty bed; the most serious incident in wartime Oxford occurred on 4 May when a Whitley bomber crashed on Mrs Haldane's gardener's cottage in Linton Road, killing the crew and badly injuring the three occupants of the house.[72] With the so-called 'Baedeker' raids on places like Bath, Canterbury and Exeter, Oxford still seemed very much at risk and the decision was taken to remove both the city and county ARP Control Centres from the city centre to the relative safety of North Oxford; the city's was relocated to Alexandra Courts in Summertown and the county's to Blandford Avenue.[73] The lowest basement of the New Bodleian Library was converted into an air-raid shelter for up to 1,100 by July 1942. A night guard of thirty people slept at the Bodleian and two thousand of the

German aerial reconnaissance photograph taken in September 1940 to highlight the Morris Radiators factory in Woodstock Road as a strategic target.

library's greatest treasures were removed to the underground galleries of a stone quarry near Bath.[74]

These efforts proved unnecessary, however, and throughout the county, as in Benson, ARP was 'a constant preparation against air attack, which mercifully never came'.[75] It has been claimed that, on 30 August 1940, a formation of Heinkel 111 bombers was sent to destroy the Oxford factories only to be intercepted over Surrey and turned back.[76] No further raids seem to have been launched against these important targets and the city's escape from 'Baedeker' raids has never been satisfactorily explained. Speculation has suggested that Hitler envisaged Blenheim Palace as a convenient seat of government for a Nazi Britain or, more plausibly perhaps, that Oxford was spared because it would have been a vital centre of communications in the event of an invasion.[77] No bombs fell in Oxfordshire from August 1941 until three unexploded bombs were deposited on the southern edge of Broadwell airfield in April 1944; later in the summer, four V1s landed in the Henley area, but the county was beyond the range of the V2 rockets.[78] In these circumstances, it proved increasingly difficult to maintain a universal commitment to air-raid precautions. The log-book of Post J93 at 116 Lime Walk, Headington, recorded just forty-eight alerts between March 1942 and August 1944 and only a few problems with breaches of the black-out at Park Hospital; a warden was particularly suspicious on 22 May 1942:

> Windows of nurse's bedroom without any curtains drawn; could not at first be extinguished because the door was locked. Key at last 'borrowed' and light put out at 23.15. (Nurse Schreiber).[79]

Burford had only 162 alerts during the entire war and its nearest stray bomb fell a quarter of a mile away near the Oxford road. At Kingham four bombs landed near the Black Bridge on 3 April 1941 and the bungalow belonging to the Hall family was damaged, although Mrs Hall 'was more concerned over her jars of jam being broken than about anything else'; the people of Islip spoke almost proprietorially about 'Our Bomb' which damaged two farm cottages and killed a pig.[80] Some fire crews were drafted into heavily bombed cities at the height of the Blitz and, on 10 May 1941, for example, Burford firemen were called to assist in London; crews from the National Fire Service in Oxford were summoned to London, Coventry, Bristol and Manchester during 1940 and 1941.[81]

For most ARP personnel a life of watching and waiting was relieved only by exercises like the role-playing demonstration at Banbury on 9 May 1943. Among the incidents which local officials acted out was one where an indignant lady comes to report 'bomb damage':

> 'My house suffered from last night's raid and I want repairs carried out immediately. I have had a shocking night and I insist that my house be given immediate attention.'
>
> 'What is the extent of the damage?'
>
> 'Well, as a matter of fact, I am not quite sure, but the windows are blown out and I simply detest draughts.'
>
> 'The windows will be replaced automatically as soon as possible.'
>
> 'When will they be replaced, if it rains my furniture will be ruined?'

'Will you kindly move along please as there are persons here in greater need than you. I assure you the matter will be attended to upon your reporting it to the table marked "Borough Surveyor".'[82]

Reading was one answer to the tedium and, in Oxford, the City Librarian tried to facilitate this by circulating batches of books around the wardens' posts. The books themselves became a problem at Post C31 (St Hugh's College) as C.M. Seddon recorded in the log-book in 1939:

Oct 29th. Yesterday I took 5 library books to Post C32 because I was informed that that Post had rung up for them. At Post C32 Miss Andrews, who was on duty, told me that her Post had sent these 5 books to us & of course did not want them back. She also said her Post had only received 5 books & not 6 & had sent the 5 to us. So, if there is any question of one book being missing the fault is not ours. The 5 books are now here again as I brought them back. As soon as we hear who really wants them we can send them.[83]

No such luxury was available at Wootton near Woodstock where, during the winter of 1940, wardens 'went to their posts, and then just waited through the hours of the night, trying to keep warm, and listening to the approaching and receding drone of many planes far overhead, wondering if they were enemy planes or our own'.[84] The inactivity proved too much for one warden at the Bartons:

The first members of Royal Observer Corps Group Y1.1212, the Shipton-under-Wychwood post. Reg Bradley, on the left, was the Head Observer.

One night at midnight when the wardens and First Aid party were at their headquarters, some playing cards, others sitting around, they heard a series of bangs and rushed out to their posts. They found nothing and when the chief warden came back he found one warden half asleep. He had not gone out he said as he had not heard the bangs or the order, and then it transpired that the noise had been made by his nodding head hitting against the wooden boards. The remarks that followed cannot of course be printed.[85]

ARP posts were sometimes far from comfortable, and N.K. Wells, one of the wardens at Post C31 in St Hugh's College lodge, was moved to verse by its short-comings when 24-hour manning ended in November 1939:

'He serveth most who loveth most
All things both great and small'
And so I leave the little Post
I have not loved at all.

It was a horrid little Post
Dirty and Damp and small
And yet (I do not wish to boast)
I think perhaps I served it most,
If hours count – of all.

And now you are to close – Poor Post
Unless the Hun's bombs fall
And may your dirty little ghost
Be honoured one day with the toast
'It never was used at all.'[86]

It is not surprising in these circumstances that some people began to evade compulsory but seemingly unnecessary firewatching duties at the end of the working day. In April 1943 an Abingdon man was sent to prison for a month for failing to attend firewatching, having been fined for a previous offence. Eight factory workers were fined for the same offence at Oxford in October; one had signed on at Osberton Radiators just before 8 p.m. and then slipped away, being observed returning through a hedge at 5.30 a.m.[87]

For the most part, the efficiency of the ARP services in the Oxford area was not therefore subjected to the full rigours of enemy attack. Perhaps this was just as well at Chinnor in July 1940:

The 'burning question of the day' in Chinnor concerns the control of the new fire-fighting unit. It seems that the stirrup pump acquired by the utility squad of the ARP quite satisfied that body's fiery zeal until it became known that an energetic member of the Parish Council had subsequently obtained the promise of a real fire-engine in the near future, whereupon a hot controversy broke out to decide whether the fire-engine shall be manned and controlled (especially the latter) by the utility squad or by the Parish Council. As neither faction apparently owns a two-headed half-penny, both are unwilling to toss for it. In the meantime it is warmly hoped that enemy aircraft will tactfully refrain from dropping any incendiary bombs in the district until the dissension has burnt itself out, one way or the other.[88]

Things seem to have been little better in Witney in September 1941 when between eighty and ninety members of the ARP services signed a resolution criticizing the degree of disharmony between certain sections and individuals and between Control and the various services.[89] In Oxford at the end of January 1943, Exercise Carfax or the Battle of Oxford was a major test of civil defence efficiency and found it was wanting in several respects. Area reports on the approaches to Magdalen Bridge stated that 'Fire Guards, particularly women, showed much enthusiasm but were sadly lacking in training'; in Union Street the wardens were bad with 'traffic allowed over UXB (unexploded bomb) and conference held on top of the said bomb'. Some of the worst criticism was reserved for North Oxford:

I am afraid that I am unable to report favourably on the Service. There appeared to be entire lack of leadership which resulted in a considerable amount of arguing. No Incident Control was observed and very little reconnaissance of incidents was made. . . . There were instances of wardens standing about without making any attempt to contact each other. No attention to casualties pending arrival of Services was made and when they did arrive, no warden was detailed to meet and guide them to the incident.

The general opinion, however, was that the exercise had been a good one and the County ARP Controller expressed confidence that 'had the real thing taken place the work done by all services would have been even more efficient than it was'. Unfortunately, the city had already taken umbrage about some of the reports and Major Scott's barbed comments about the City Controller having too many staff and being reluctant to delegate routine matters did nothing to improve relations between the two authorities.[90]

If ARP perhaps failed to achieve perfect efficiency in the comparatively untroubled conditions of wartime Oxfordshire, the services undoubtedly built up a team spirit which would have been vitally important in the event of major air raids. This camaraderie survived the gradual run-down towards the end of the war as the black-out was replaced by a dim-out on 17 September 1944, car headlights shone out again on Christmas Eve and public clocks were illuminated by the beginning of 1945.[91] An almost perverse enjoyment in troubles shared and overcome was evident in the series of ARP RIP dinners which were held in Oxford from 1944. The menus, one disguised as an Abdominal Refilling Programme Training Manual, recalled the service jargon for the bombs and other deadly weapons which were no longer a threat:

Soup
Creme de Poule Allclear

Entree
Salmon Anti-personnel
Sauce Mayonnaise à la Marygold

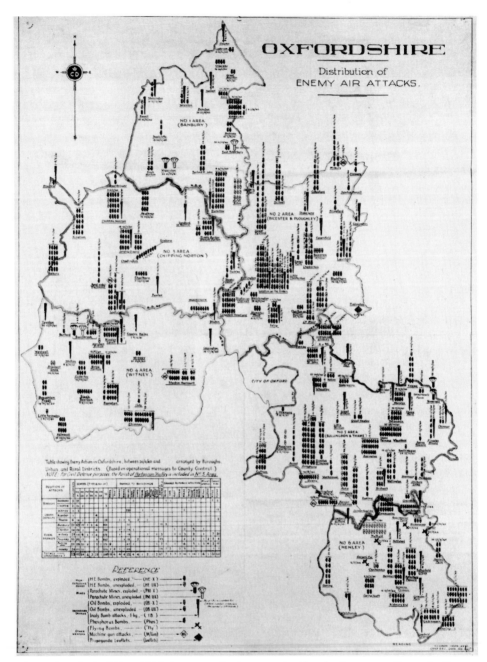

Air raids in Oxfordshire, 1940–4; a map plotting every incident in the county, from a leaflet drop at Piddington to the landing of four V1s in South Oxfordshire.

OR
Hamm à la Marshalling Yard
Tongue Telephone
Salad Debris
Bombes de Terre UXB

Sweets
Fruit Jelly Mobile
Trifle Camouflet
Glace Most Secret
Gateau Donovan

Persistent Cheese

Café Alert[92]

For the ordinary person the end of the black-out was an enormous psychological boost and, when some of Henley's street lights were re-lit in September 1944, the *Henley Standard* reported: 'In the Market Place and at the Cross there was quite an appreciable crowd and there were subdued cheers as the lights came on.'[93] At the end of the war, one of the most memorable things for F.P. Chamberlain at Benson was being able once again to see 'light showing from cottage windows at night'.[94]

CHAPTER THREE

Evacuees

Government plans for evacuation evolved in 1938 as a response to the threat that war would swiftly lead to massive air raids and severe civilian casualties. The country was divided into evacuation, reception and neutral areas with Oxfordshire being designated as a reception area. Host families were promised payment for taking in evacuees and, early in 1939, a census was carried out to establish how much accommodation was available. In Oxford 22,600 houses were visited and, on the basis of one person per room, the city was given a theoretical capacity of 31,000 evacuees. Nevertheless, the Chief Sanitary Officer had to report nil returns from 904 houses where his staff had found nobody at home or householders had refused to supply the necessary information. Didcot Parish Council refused to cooperate with the survey, arguing that the area was unsuitable for evacuees. The census was therefore imperfect, but it enabled the Ministry of Health to allocate numbers of evacuees to each local authority area and Oxford, for example, was asked to take 20,000, a figure that was later reduced to 12,550 because of transport difficulties and the anticipated demand for billets by the military and civil servants.[1] Banbury Borough was warned to expect 2,600 evacuees and Banbury Rural District 2,200.[2]

Local authorities throughout the country made the necessary preparations and, when the crisis deepened as Germany invaded Poland on 1 September 1939, the first trainloads of evacuees were brought to Oxfordshire. Many London schoolchildren had rehearsed for such an occasion and nine-year-old Bill Harwood had little time to prepare:

> It was a rush job. We were sent to school and we were sent home to get our parcels and we were off. That was the Friday morning about 10 o'clock. You didn't know what to expect, I mean, the thought of going to the countryside was something out of the ordinary, I mean, you know what London's like, especially the East End of London, but of course when we did go and we was parted from our parents that was a different proposition.

Bill Harwood joined his classmates with their brown paper packages, food parcels, gas masks and identity labels, and, in a scene repeated on so many other railway platforms, they were seen off by their parents to a destination unknown. Another evacuee recalled her feelings as a ten-year-old:

> I didn't really realize what the war was and I had a carrier bag full of food and I imagined that that was going to be my food for the duration of the war.[3]

A trainload of evacuees from West Ham arrives at Chipping Norton railway station. The children were given tea in the New Cinema and were then taken to their billets in the town.

The first train to reach Banbury arrived with 800 children and 80 teachers from schools in the West Ham, Camberwell and Dagenham Districts:

As the train drew into the station there were many faces at every window, and all the kiddies seemed anxious to get glimpses of this new town they were being brought to.

Many of the smaller ones, obviously with memories of Sunday school outings fresh in their minds, seemed to expect a glimpse of the sea. One youngster, as he was helped down from his carriage, was heard to ask 'Is this a seaside town, guv'nor?'

There were friendly smiles from the station staff and the local helpers on the platform, and there were no tears among the 800 young evacuees as they lined up on the platform.

Each carried luggage firmly in one hand and cardboard boxed gas masks in the other, and every child was complete with a clearly marked label, securely tied on, to prevent any confusion. There was plenty of chatter as the teachers, with a world of tact and friendly smiles marshalled the various groups on the platform.

With just a bag of belongings and a gas mask in a cardboard box, a young evacuee leads his sister out of Oxford station and into an unknown world.

There was absolutely no confusion. In a very few minutes the train was empty – except for a profusion of orange peel and discarded chocolate wrappings.

A fleet of buses soon took the children away to be billeted in Bloxham, Adderbury, Deddington and other nearby villages.[4]

Elsewhere in the county, thousands of evacuees were arriving at Oxford station and quiet afternoons at Chipping Norton, Charlbury and Culham stations were suddenly enlivened as special trains drew in. At Bicester the billeting 'went like clockwork' according to one evacuee, the future comedian Kenneth Williams,[5] and the joint efforts of the Chief Evacuation Officer, Stewart Swift, and the stationmaster, Frank Buckingham, ensured that everything ran smoothly at Oxford station:

There was practically no confusion or congestion and there was very little delay between the time children arrived on the platform and when they boarded the buses for the distribution centres.[6]

'Blimey,' cried one East London boy, 'they don't 'arf 'ave some good buses in this place.' Seventy-five of his fellow evacuees were probably less impressed after their bus became ignominiously stuck below the notorious Botley Road railway bridge.[7] In fact, this incident was just one of many that brought elements of chaos and even farce into this sudden, large-scale transfer of population. Congestion on the railways, for example, made some trains hours late and the last one only reached Oxford at 7 p.m.:

Up to a late hour dozens of children, who were practically 'all-in' after a long day, were still being walked from house to house, and in parts of East Oxford some of the teachers were still trying at 12.30 a.m. to get a bed for the night.[8]

In other instances trains failed to reach their intended destinations as Bill Harwood remembered.

We were told we were going to Banbury and I really thought we were going to Banbury. When we asked what particular place we were going, Banbury was the word mentioned. I had never heard of Banbury in my life, I'd never heard of Oxford in my life. You know, we thought Banbury was the place but things change, I don't know if it was meant to be or if it was just one of those particular things, but we didn't get to Banbury, we got to Oxford.[9]

At Woodcote welcoming villagers were dismayed by the arrival of mothers and babies who should have gone to Tring, and Benson received from Oxford station a group of evacuees who were meant to be in Weston-super-Mare.[10] Wantage took in children from West Ham, Plaistow and Bow, the two departments from West Ham arriving quite by accident:

They should have gone to Somerset, with other West Ham schools, but being provided by the railway company with a non-corridor train the needs of nature proved too strong and they had to be deposited at Wantage.[11]

These last-minute changes disrupted the plans of local billeting officers and, at Charlbury for example, helpers awaiting 113 London schoolchildren and teachers

Mrs Powell and other helpers lead evacuated children through Corn Street, Witney, at the outbreak of war.

on 2 September were belatedly informed that three bus-loads of pregnant women and mothers with babies were on their way from Chipping Norton. A loudspeaker van was sent round the village in a desperate search for more accommodation and boy scouts took messages to the larger houses, appealing for hospitality and the use of cars. The 170 tired evacuees arrived at 7 p.m. and proved very difficult to house because unrealistic promises had been made that each family would be able to stay together:

> This gave rise to some awkward problems, such as the housing of a mother accompanied by six children under seven and their grandmother. This whole party was accommodated at Sandford Mount, the children bedded down on mattresses on the floor. . . . Another party of fifteen related mothers and children refused to separate and said they would rather sleep on bare boards at the school and return to London the next day. It was 10.15 p.m. before they were persuaded to go to several houses in the same row in Woodstock Road.[12]

Even when evacuees arrived as planned it was not always easy to accommodate them. At Tetsworth and Littlemore, for example, some evacuees had to be housed temporarily by Viscountess Harcourt and the authorities at Radley College;[13] in Oxford some of the colleges were brought into use as emergency billets.[14] A girls' school evacuated from London to Botley spent the first night at Hill End Camp before local residents arrived to make their selection with comments like 'Could I have that one?' or 'I like the look of that girl'. The girls who remained had to be ferried by bus to Kennington because there were no other places in Botley and one of their teachers found accommodation equally elusive:

> It was very haphazard. . . . At the end of the first day I had nowhere to sleep. I had to go with one girl who had and stay the night with her and then the next day we walked up Cumnor Hill and the Deputy Head saw a man painting a house [and said] will you have an evacuee, a teacher, and he said yes, and I went there. I was there three and a half years as happy as anything. They were very kind.[15]

By 6 September the population of Oxford and Oxfordshire had been swollen by 19,830 official evacuees.[16] This figure was considerably lower than the original allocation and, at Banbury, the Clerk to the Rural District Council, Mr E.L. Fisher, had good reason to be displeased because only 1,120 evacuees had arrived instead of the anticipated 2,200. He explained that the Government was supposed to provide blankets for them,

> but shortly before the first batch of evacuees arrived he had had a message telling him to obtain as many blankets as he could from anywhere. He succeeded in purchasing the last 400 blankets left at Witney Mill for 10s. each, and a number of ladies helped with the work of making mattresses for the children. Shortly after the evacuation had taken place blankets appeared to come from everywhere. The Government sent 2,500, and as it was only necessary to issue 530 in addition to the 400 already sent out, there were now over 2,000 left in storage.[17]

Evacuees put on a brave face for the photographer at an unknown village hall.

The shortfall of official evacuees was, to some extent, made up by the arrival of other refugees who had made their own arrangements. On the eve of war, the Billeting Officer for Fulbrook recalled the stream of traffic along the A40:

I got the impression of endless cars, laden high with luggage, fleeing westwards from the 'wrath to come', the drivers ever looking backwards over their shoulders. It was uneasy and uncanny.[18]

Some of these private evacuees were simply returning to the county to stay with relatives, one example being an unfortunate woman who travelled down from London to Upper Heyford on 1 September only to be killed in a road accident the following day at Hopcroft's Holt.[19] At Tadmarton the rapport which developed between a foster parent and her young evacuee from the East End led to the rest of his family being invited to join them[20] and there were probably other occasions when official evacuation led to a more extensive exodus.

Many people found themselves living in Oxfordshire because their school or place of work was evacuated to the area. Radley College shared its premises with Eastbourne College and Lord Faringdon moved into his lodge so that the girls of Ancaster House School from Bexhill could occupy Buscot Park.[21] Malvern College was commandeered to house the Admiralty in case London was heavily bombed and, in the circumstances, the school was grateful to accept the Duke of

"Balliol may be a bit earlier, but this is one of the oldest Ministries in the University."

A 1943 cartoon depicting civil servants in the Front Quad of Corpus Christi College.

Marlborough's offer of Blenheim Palace. It opened in these unusual surroundings within just five weeks of the outbreak of war, during which time movable treasures were removed from the palace and stored, and other things such as pictures and tapestries were protected. The enormous windows, some up to 60 ft high, had to be blacked out, and huge quantities of furniture and equipment had to be moved from Malvern:

> Practically all the transport at this time, certainly in the Midlands, was under Government control, and consequently the services of the local firms were secured for us by the Ministry of Works. This relieved us of one great anxiety, but caused us another, for although we were spared the trouble and expense of securing vans and labour, we had no control over the movements of the vans or the work of the men. We watched with apprehension the loading up, which was carried out at break-neck speed. At Blenheim we had to be ready at all hours of the day to direct the contents as they arrived at the Palace steps to their proper destination, and the final blow came when on the second day the men announced that they had received orders to dump the [fifty-five] van-loads on the steps and return to Malvern with the utmost speed.

The school operated until July 1940 in a surrealistic combination of palatial rooms and hutted classrooms built in the main courtyard, but was then able to return home because bomb-proof bunkers had been completed for the various Whitehall departments.[22] Blenheim, like Cornbury Park, was subsequently taken over by the War Office.[23] London University medical students had taken over

Women clerks at St John's College in November 1939. Their 'invasion' of a masculine world followed the general exodus of businesses and Government Departments to the comparative safety of Oxford and Oxfordshire.

Keble College, Wadham College and St Peter's Hall by October 1939. Government departments soon established offices in several Oxford colleges and, within days of the outbreak of war, the Director of Fish Supplies from the Board of Trade was ensconced in St John's College, causing Oxford to be described as 'the centre of the fishing industry'. Chatham House, the Royal Institute of International Affairs, was housed in Balliol College and, by November, the University was said to have been transformed by 'a feminine invasion' of women clerks.[24] Elsewhere, Oaken Holt at Farmoor was acquired by the Westminster Bank, Chesterton House by the Royal Exchange, Bucknell Manor by the BBC and Milton Hill House by the Anglo-American Oil Company.[25] The county's most distinguished 'evacuee' was, however, the Prime Minister, Winston Churchill, who spent weekends at Ditchley 'when the moon was high' and Chequers was in danger of being bombed. While Churchill and his entourage were staying with Ronald and Nancy Tree, the house was guarded by soldiers of the Oxfordshire and Buckinghamshire Light Infantry and 'scrambler' telephones were installed. In January 1943 Churchill left Ditchley to fly from RAF Stanton Harcourt on his way to the Casablanca conference with Roosevelt and Stalin.[26]

The sudden influx of population into Oxfordshire created major concerns in the fields of education and health provision. By the autumn of 1939 the Education Department of Oxfordshire County Council had 58 per cent more children on its books than it had had in July.[27] Extra children were crowded into most local schools and Whitchurch, for example, received sixty-two evacuees from Westville Road School in London while Cumnor was joined by pupils from West Silvertown and Atlay Road School.[28] The Wesleyan Methodist School in Witney added sixty-four evacuees from West Ham and elsewhere to its usual complement of 108 children. In Oxford schools evacuated from Hammersmith and Poplar found themselves sharing 'The Poplars' with Pressed Steel's ARP Headquarters.[29] The shortage of accommodation in Bicester became so acute that Bignell House was requisitioned in February 1941 for the senior and junior departments of two London schools, leaving the infant and nursery classes to use the Wesley and Gospel Halls in the town. At its peak Bignell Park Evacuated School had over 200 children who were brought in by bus from Bicester every day. In 1945 His Majesty's Inspector reported:

> The staff was faced with a big creative undertaking, but it rose admirably to the occasion and from the first, the novel enterprise took a most happy turn under the dual Headship of the West Ham Headmaster [Edward Hart], a man of genial and live personality, and the LCC Headmistress [Miss G.M. Merrivale] in charge of the LCC girls. Day to day difficulties were taken in their stride, Esprit de Corps was established, and no doubt the successful school dinner

A group from the Slade School of Fine Art on the steps of the Ashmolean Museum in June 1943. The Slade was evacuated from London and found a temporary home in Oxford.

arrangement added to the happiness of the school life as did the enjoyment of the beautiful and spacious open-air surroundings in which the children were able to disport themselves.[30]

If schooling provided one area of concern the increased numbers of young mothers also required the establishment of emergency maternity homes. At the outbreak of war Oxford city and county took over Ruskin College and Campsfield House, Kidlington, for the purpose but, probably because the latter was needed to house RAF personnel, it was replaced as a maternity home from September 1940 by Davenport House in Headington Hill, Oxford.[31] In May 1940 the county was instructed by the Ministry of Health to open another maternity hospital for evacuees at Chippinghurst Manor,[32] and Berkshire County Council provided similar facilities at Oakley House and Frilford St Peter in Frilford Heath.[33]

Pressure on local services diminished a little during the winter of 1939–40 as the 'Phoney War' encouraged many evacuees to return to their homes. Mothers with very young children were generally the keenest to go back, prompted by unhappiness and, in some cases, by financial necessity because their contribution to the family income was essential. Some women found it

Lessons among the tapestries for boys from Malvern College at Blenheim Palace. After its buildings were commandeered for the Admiralty, the college spent the first year of the war in these memorable surroundings.

very difficult to share cooking and washing facilities with another household,[34] and others like 'A London Mother' were simply disgusted by their billets:

> As an evacuated London mother, I am writing in the hope that one of your readers may know of a decent home for my little girl and myself. I am not very strong and my husband was pleased for us to come away, as he thought we should be well looked after, instead of which we are right in the slums of Oxford. When I think of my pretty home in London, I feel I should get the next train back; in fact, I had decided to go this week, but the thought of my little girl being in danger makes me hesitate. . . . [She] is just four years and I could not expose her to the dangers of an air-raid, but I feel at the end of my resources, and I feel I cannot go on unless I can get out of this place. My child has not had a bath since we came here on 2 September, as there is nothing to bath her in. The total absence of privacy makes life a torture to me.[35]

By Christmas 1939 no mothers with young children were left in Burford[36], and at the beginning of 1940 the number of evacuees in Banbury and Witney Rural Districts had been cut by half.[37]

The fall of France in May 1940 and the imminent threat of invasion prompted a second movement of population. Emigration was an option for a few and, in June, the *Bicester Advertiser* publicized a Government scheme which offered free passage and a home in the Dominions for children aged between five and sixteen.[38] At the same time, the children of Oxford and Cambridge dons were invited by Yale and Toronto Universities and private individuals to take refuge in Canada and the United States. A group of 125 children and 25 mothers left Oxford station on 8 July and, for some fathers, a written farewell had to suffice. This is the letter which four-year-old Martin Hugh-Jones received:

> LONDON
> JUNE 25TH
> 1940
>
> DARLING BOY
> THIS IS A LITTLE NOTE
> TO BRING YOU YOUR DADDY'S
> LOVE ON YOUR BIG ADVENTURE.
> JUST SAY TO YOURSELF, WILL
> YOU, 'DADDY LOVES ME VERY
> MUCH' AND BE SURE THAT
> IT WON'T BE VERY LONG
> BEFORE THERE IS ANOTHER
> BIG SHIP FOR ALL OF US.
> ALWAYS YOUR LOVING
> DADDY
> XOXOXOXOXOXOXO
> OXOXOXOXOXOXOX

The train pulled away as parents waved and one of the children, Ann Spokes, recalled the moment of departure:

I still remember my mother in a kelly-green dress, waving from the end of the platform and recall that I was proud of the fact that she had run the fastest and thus could be seen from the window of our carriage at the end of the train long after everyone else.

One excited girl, Ellie Bourdillon, must have redoubled adult doubts about the wisdom of the enterprise:

As our train pulled away from family and friends . . . I apparently leaned out of the carriage window and called: 'Wouldn't it be fun if we were torpedoed!' I suppose this summed up the state of mind of the younger travellers – it was an adventure, fun at that stage because we were a party and leaving home hadn't made itself felt, and we had no idea how long the separation would last. One thought in round terms of 'a year or so'. In my case it was almost six years.

The train drew into Banbury after about half an hour of the long journey and five-year-old Susan Lawson asked: 'Is this Canada yet?' Eventually, the party reached Liverpool and sailed on the SS *Antonia* for Montreal the following night.[39] They reached Canada safely and were treated like celebrities as Ann Spokes recorded in her diary for Sunday 21 July:

After breakfast we had a service at 10.0 a.m. in the Common Room. We sung hymns and had a lesson and a few prayers. We had *group photos* taken on the steps of the college. Before lunch Chalky and I had a short game of tennis on the college courts. In the afternoon we were taken round the town by one of the men helping. . . . At 3.0 we assembled in the games room & got into groups of ages and then we went to Mgill [sic] University Park or field as they call it, to have a picnic. We played rounders & deck tennis, then we had tea in circles of our own groups. We had a bag each which were called grab-bags. Crowds gathered round us to watch us eat. We were going in some cabs up to the mountain after the picnic but it couldn't be arranged so we went home. Played in the gym. Two or three girls came to get our autographs – lots of fun![40]

Back in England the beginning of the London Blitz on 7 September 1940 generated a new wave of evacuees and bombed-out families. Oxford was warned three days later to expect 7,500 evacuees from Ashford in Kent, 2,700 of whom were to be housed in the city. In the event, only 5,000 came and about 1,600 stayed in Oxford, but even this reduced number required emergency accommodation in the Town Hall and several colleges including Christ Church, Balliol, Merton and Lady Margaret Hall.[41] H.W.B. Joseph noted in his diary:

Billeting is most difficult. Some families are very large, and object to separation. Many houses are still reserved for civil servants; military billeting will also come presently. Driblets of 10 or 12 still arrive daily. Unofficial evacuees to the number of 3,000–5,000 have also passed through the Majestic

Eastbourne College 1st XV in December 1943. Evacuated from the vulnerable south coast in June 1940, Eastbourne College shared the premises of Radley College for the rest of the war.

Cinema which has been a main depot (250 were there on Tuesday) and in all perhaps 7,000 have come independently. Many houses have received relatives and friends from London. The increase of city population already this month is put at between 10,000 and 15,000.[42]

The Evacuation Officer was forced to buy 5 tons of straw to fill mattresses for the huge influx of refugees at the Majestic in Botley Road.[43] This rest and feeding centre was soon overcrowded and filthy, and conditions there were described by Vera Brittain:

Amongst the rugs and perambulators on the short dry grass (outside) lie pieces of chewed apple core, fragments of orange peel, and the inevitable sheets of torn dirty newspaper which indicate, like a paper trail, the presence of an evacuee population the moment that it moves from its normal environment.

As I enter the cinema, a familiar and overpowering stench strikes me on the face like a blow. Where did I last encounter it? I wonder, and then I remember; it was the smell of the crowded Ladies' Saloon on the night boat during a rough Channel crossing. Gradually my nose becomes accustomed to it as my eyes also accommodate themselves to the unillumined twilight inside the building. Covering the floor beneath the upturned velveteen seats of the cinema chairs, disorderly piles of mattresses, pillows, rugs and cushions indicate the 'pitches' staked out by each evacuated family. Many of the women, too dispirited to move, still lie wearily on the floor with their children beside them in the foetid air, though the hour is 11 a.m. and a warm sun is shining cheerfully on the city streets. Between the mattresses and cushions, the customary collection of soiled newspapers and ancient apple cores is contributing noticeably to the odoriferous atmosphere. A few small boys, evidently set to the task by the organisers on the floor above, are making a determined attack on the extensive squalor with besoms and brooms.[44]

The wretched conditions at the Majestic led to questions in the House of Commons, but an attempt to transfer many of the occupants to Wolverhampton failed when many families refused to be split up and had to be brought back to Oxford. Finally, in January 1941, the city decided to close the building to evacuees, transferring about 250 people to Bournemouth and forcing the others to find local billets or return to London.[45]

The Blitz had similar repercussions throughout the Oxford area and, in September 1940, the *Faringdon Advertiser* noted the return of an extended family of seventeen which had been billeted in Eaton Hastings the previous year.[46] Banbury received 1,000 evacuees in three days and was forced to find temporary accommodation for some of them in the old workhouse in Warwick Road.[47] By November the population of Thame was estimated at 4,580, an increase of 1,552 over the usual figure because of the presence of so many official and private evacuees.[48] At the end of 1940 the county's Medical Officer of Health had 8,613 evacuee children on the books compared with 4,706 a year earlier.[49] Nor was

Refugees from the London Blitz in the Front Quad of University College, one of the colleges providing emergency billets in September 1940. Sir William Beveridge, then Master of the College, is the smiling figure on the left.

evacuation solely a matter for human beings when invasion was expected at any time; around Benson, sheep enjoyed comparatively safe grazing after being removed from the vulnerable area of Romney Marsh on the Sussex and Kent borders.[50]

As the war dragged on many evacuees returned to their homes and this is graphically demonstrated by the steady fall in the number of children on the county's books; there were still 7,211 in December 1941, but only 3,565 a year later and just 2,394 at the end of 1943.[51] The traffic was not entirely one way, however, and in May 1941 the County's ARP Controller reported the continuing arrival of small numbers of evacuees driven from their homes by the bombing of Plymouth and Portsmouth.[52] Oxford was still so crowded in the summer of 1943 that a man and his wife who had been bombed out of London were happy to find accommodation aboard Magdalen College barge; at Bicester the White family lived for a time in the Sports Ground tennis pavilion.[53] As late as January 1942 the Ministry of Health was warning the County Council that the special wartime nurseries at Bruern Abbey and Sandford Park in Sandford St Martin would have to take more than their approved numbers if a grave emergency required the evacuation of unaccompanied children under the age of five.[54]

During the summer of 1944 the decline in the number of evacuees was suddenly thrown into reverse as Hitler's V1s or 'Doodlebugs' were launched against London and the south-east. In July the Food Control Officer for Oxford and Bullingdon area reported that 'newcomers to Oxford during the past three weeks have averaged about 1,000 per day'; at the end of the month Henley Town Council learned that there were over 1,000 evacuees in the borough.[55] Billeting once again became a serious problem, and in Bicester a pregnant woman and her three children had to live for a time in a stable; in Eynsham an air-raid shelter provided a sort of home described for Witney Rural District Council by Father Lopes:

> There was . . . a child there who had suffered from whooping cough for three weeks. There were 17 children under five, with only three cots between them. Adults and children were sleeping on the floor. There was a permanent black-out and insufficient cooking facilities. It was the foundation of a first-class breeding ground for epidemics in the area.[56]

With the capture of the V-bomb sites in Northern France by the Allies in September 1944 this crisis was short-lived and mass evacuation came gradually to an end.

Children had in fact proved remarkably adaptable to the upheavals of evacuation and many of them settled down happily in their new surroundings. They were undoubtedly helped by the policy of trying to keep whole schools together so that children usually remained with their friends and teachers. Thus, a party of thirty children and teachers from Enfield spent eighteen happy months at Leafield from June 1940:

> These teachers entered so whole heartedly into the work of the school and the social life of the village that it was to the great regret of all that eventually they were recalled to London. The most astonishing feature of the evacuation was

the rapidity with which the town children were absorbed into the life of the school and the village. They never regarded themselves as strangers or formed independent isolated factions, but for the time became Leafield children.[57]

Jonathan Webb, a nine-year-old Londoner, was evacuated with his family to North Dean near High Wycombe after their home was bombed while they were taking refuge in their Anderson shelter. He delighted in the change, recalling that 'I was drunk, I was drunk with the countryside for about three months. I went round in a state of euphoria.'[58] Some of the children evacuated to Oxford enjoyed the scenery, the walks and the river[59] and the county's School Medical Officer was able to testify to the improved health of many evacuees by the end of 1939:

> There has been a marked improvement in the general condition of many of the children. In some cases it is reported that there has been a marked increase in weight, and it is generally admitted that the majority of the children look better and are more alert after their comparatively short stay in the country. This is no doubt largely due to the quieter life which they lead, regular food, and what is probably of most importance, regular and adequate sleep.[60]

To some evacuees, however, a quieter life was an extremely dull one and the bus to Oxford proved to be a lifeline for those billeted at Sandford St Martin:

> The evacuees staying in the village never failed to take advantage of it, but what struck me so forcibly was that they also went on Sundays, so I enquired of one young woman in the course of casual conversation, if they had friends in Oxford as they went so regularly.
> 'Oh no,' she said, 'you see we go to see the shops in the week and on Sundays we go to the Park. There's such a nice park in Oxford.'
> 'But,' said I, 'there are lovely walks and parks here.'
> 'Oh,' the lady replied, 'but there ain't no folks to see. We likes to watch the folks and see the fashions; here there's only fields.'[61]

The lack of social facilities in the villages around Wantage left older girls with 'so much time on their hands that they were able to devote a great deal of it to the village lads, with considerable effect'; teachers at Botley faced a similar problem with a forward girl and 'we used to do the policing on the Hurst when we knew she was up there'.[62] In Bicester a few of the older boys, accustomed to earning money by spare time occupations in London, resorted to petty crime, stealing bikes and shoplifting.[63]

Some children found it difficult to adjust to country life where there were 'funny horses' with horns, and apples grew on trees; one child indignantly refused fresh milk saying, 'we haven't our milk from a dirty cow, we have it from a clean bottle'.[64] Others, like a seven-year-old girl at Bicester, had to cope with new standards of behaviour:

> She had never seen a knife and fork before and she ate with her fingers. She was used to sleeping under the table with a pet monkey. She still wet the bed at 6. She was a very frail, thin child who had been undernourished, but she was

very brave. Her parents used to come down every few months to see her. They were a bit of nuisance because they would first get drunk in the 'Plough'.[65]

In Oxfordshire children were never far from their parents, and in December 1939 a special 'parents' express' was organized to bring London parents to Oxford.[66] A young evacuee in Bicester recorded one such visit in 1941 in loving detail:

> My mother came the Monday after Easter, also my friend's mother and father. We went to meet them at eleven o'clock. My mother had brought us a lot of things, so she had a big case. She unpacked the case before dinner so that we could go out all the afternoon. My mother had made my sister and myself a two-piece, it was a pink frock and coatee of pink stripes for best, also a frock each for school. For my lady she brought a pound of dates, some butter which she had not used, some cooking apples and oranges. We had a two-pound tin of sweets and six pounds of chocolates, which were milk chocolates between us, which we had to try to keep. My lady had a pound of sweets and chocolate. When we had put them all away, we had our dinner. After dinner we called for our friend with her mother and father. We planned to go for a long walk across the fields. When we had gone a good way we sat in the fields, and played ball. The time passed very quickly and it was half past four. We started walking back as it was tea time at five o'clock. On the way back we saw some soldiers drilling up and down the street. For tea we had some chocolate biscuits which my mother brought for us. After tea we had a rest and read until half past six, then we started walking to the station. We just got there in time, for the train was just going off.[67]

More often, contact was maintained by letter and Mrs D. Warner, the former postmistress at Ascott-under-Wychwood, recalled that, after they had been evacuated to the village in September 1939, 'about fifty poor frightened little children . . . hung around the Post Office for days hoping for a letter from "Our Mam"'.[68] Joyce Bonsall, an eight-year-old evacuated from Bethnal Green to Arncott with her sister, received this letter from her mother after Christmas in 1939:

> Dear Joyce
>
> Thank you very much for you letter and Mummy and Daddy are very glad you liked your dolls bed what Daddy made you also the frock and sweets I hope you are still well and happy with Mrs Newell who is good to you and I hope you are a good little girl for her Well Ronnie sends you his love also Mummy and Daddy so will say Cheerio for now and may God Bless you my Darling Love from Mummy
>   very pleased to know that you had a lovely time Xmas and Boxing Day don't foreget to drink all your milk up at school Darling
>   X X X X X[69]

One child evacuee remarked bravely that 'In Oxford we have learnt to depend on ourselves instead of our parents which will be a great help in life'.[70] For most

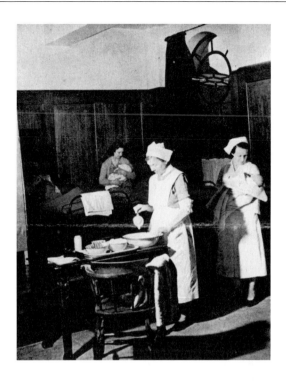

Ruskin College Maternity Home in Walton Street, Oxford, in 1939. One of the emergency maternity homes established to cope with the influx of women evacuees, Ruskin was the birthplace of over 2,500 babies between September 1939 and May 1945.

children, however, evacuation was probably a matter of *Profit and Loss*, the title of a piece by B. Jarvis, an eleven-year-old in Class 4B at Bignell Park Evacuated School:

> Coming from London I have lost my home and my old pals. I miss all the old games like 'Knocking Down Ginger' and games like that. I miss the Speedway, and all the big Football Matches. I also miss the trams and buses, and the rush and bustle in the dirty, smoky, busy market place. Of course I miss the noise that comes from the factories.
>
> I have gained some new pals and a new home. I play about in the fields and near the trees. The food I eat is all grown near, and is fresh. I have grown stronger and am in better health. I play new games and have left the danger behind.[71]

How well were the evacuees received by local residents? Many people recognized and sympathized with their plight and in June 1940, for instance, large crowds lined the station approach as special trains brought hundreds of children to Banbury:

> Mothers, who have not yet known the agony of parting with their children in such circumstances, stood in little groups, moved to pity for the long procession of cheerful youngsters. Their parents in London, now a city robbed of the cheering and friendly company of its youth, can rest assured that their children will be well cared for. One mother of four summed up the situation for an 'Advertiser' reporter. 'Our hearts go out to the parents of these children,' she

said. 'I know how badly I would suffer if I had to part with my children, and I think it is up to us to make them as happy and comfortable as possible – as a compensation for all they have had to leave behind.'[72]

A real bond of affection developed between many children and their foster parents; at Arncott Mr and Mrs Newell came to love Joyce, June and Ronnie Bonsall as the children they had never had. For their part, the girls began to call them Mum and Dad and continued to visit them for many years.[73] Local people in Bladon tried to foster a family atmosphere by running a regular social club for evacuees in the Methodist chapel.[74] In Banbury the initiative of two women, Miss Somers and Miss Cherry, led in May 1941 to the opening of Cherry House, a social club where evacuee mothers could relax, have a bath for threepence or an afternoon cup of tea for a penny. According to one of the mothers, they had previously

sat in the park during the cold weather, so that the people on whom they were billeted could 'have their home to themselves for a few hours', although they weren't made to feel in the way, she added, because she was lucky in having a 'good billet'. The club had simplified all this, and had supplied a 'comfortable place of their own' where they could knit, sew, or just rest.[75]

If most Oxfordshire people did their best to welcome the evacuees, others adopted a more hostile attitude. Around Wantage there were snide comments that

Keep smiling! An Oxford foster mother in Observatory Street seems undaunted by her 'family' of nine London evacuees.

only the 'hysterical type' of woman had been evacuated and that 'a decent woman would never leave her husband'.[76] Evacuees in Abingdon were accused of using the 'pavements and shop doorways as public lavatories'[77] and the writer of an anonymous letter to the Mayor of Oxford in 1940 clearly felt that the city should take no more:

Dr Sir

They say they say there are 7,000 Children coming down to Oxon dont have that lot here they are overcrowding there's shelters up there and this is all open and besides every week there is a case in the Junerville about the unruly things breaking the Law let them that have children look after them we have the same chance as them and see how they runs away then says people turns them out

from 1 that knows[78]

Inevitably perhaps some evacuees were exploited in their hour of need, and in September 1940 there were ugly stories of profiteering with refugees in Oxford being charged £10 for an iron bedstead, 50s a week for bed and breakfast, 2s 6d for a chair to sit in for the night and even 6d for the use of a cup and saucer.[79] When accommodation was at a premium, householders might be tempted to oust official evacuees in favour of private ones who could be charged a much higher rent.[80] In addition, there were accusations that residents in the larger houses of North Oxford and Cumnor Hill were refusing to accept evacuees and that the billeting authorities were not using compulsory powers against them;[81] a contemporary survey of evacuation in the Wantage area confirmed that

only a minority of the owners of larger houses were willing to receive evacuees. Many took it for granted that they should be sent to the smaller houses, their estimation of the weekly payments being that they were of value to the working class but not worth consideration by them. One or two had filled their houses with relatives of their servants, and so could claim that they had no available accommodation. Another, we were told by a villager, had avoided evacuees by saying that she was reserving her house for air-raid casualties. As they are extremely unlikely in such a place she will probably go on living undisturbed.

This apparent selfishness was to some extent justified by the tendency for 'children to be happiest in homes of about their own social level' and, in Wantage at least, there were attempts to put children into 'appropriate' billets from the very start.[82] The behaviour of a few evacuees certainly encouraged prejudice, and a householder in Charlbury complained that more damage had been done to his house within twelve hours of receiving evacuees than had occurred in the previous eighteen years of married life.[83] Relations between landlords and evacuees were sometimes fraught and an Appeals Tribunal set up in Oxford dealt with over 200 disputes in the first four months of its existence.[84] Hostels had to be provided for unbilletable evacuees at, for example, the old Grammar School in Henley, Maitlands at Sonning Common and Corner Cottage in Shiplake.[85] In Oxford the City Council made available a condemned house in East Oxford where Mrs Laws from Chelsea Open Air Nursery School undertook play therapy among difficult and neurotic children. She worked with children up to the age of eight and told an *Oxford Mail* reporter:

I let them choose what they will do, I don't push them. They have to have security and to know that I will never turn and rend them as others would. They can then show what they are feeling and be cured. One of the problems is to get out their fantasy and to find out what is happening. I provide an impartial background, not a pedagogue, moral attitude. It is not my business to be roused by their tempers. I want them to play out their innermost thoughts. Some children are suffering intensely. They are extremely jealous of a younger child who has been left behind with their mother in London. They paint the most dramatic picture in which all kinds of calamities are allowed to overtake the victim of their jealousy. Others show their own fears and maladjustment. After a time they will come on to really constructive play.[86]

For these children, evacuation had contributed to psychological distress; for a few others, the act of plucking them to the supposed safety of Oxfordshire ultimately proved fatal and they were killed in tragic and deeply ironic accidents. One victim was a six-year-old boy from Poplar who was killed in his bed in Stanway Road, Oxford, in September 1939 when a dummy bomb fell from an RAF bomber and crashed through the roof; another was a little girl seventeen months old who was killed by a falling bookcase at the Bruern Abbey emergency nursery in December 1941.[87] Against these sad outcomes there was clear evidence that evacuation had done much to broaden the horizons of both the evacuees and their foster parents.[88] The main intention of the Government's scheme had, however, been encapsulated in the saying 'Keep them happy, keep them safe', and for most evacuees, this was achieved. As Edward Hart, the Headmaster of Bignell Park Evacuated School, said in 1943: 'Evacuation saved many lives – it was a success from that one view alone.'[89]

CHAPTER FOUR

The Military Presence

Oxfordshire lay well behind the front line and therefore was used extensively by the armed forces for training, for stockpiling and for rest and recuperation. For six years it was a part of Fortress Britain, preparing at first for an invasion that seemed almost inevitable and then witnessing the gradual build-up which culminated in D-Day and the final defeat of Hitler. Military activity was almost omnipresent throughout the county, and even in a village like Leafield, which suffered no damage at all from bombing,

> the surrounding district was very much changed. Large tracks [sic] of land had their hedges removed and stone walls flattened. Hangars appeared and we became in the midst of many aerodromes and their satellites. Much to our sorrow numbers of trees were cut down from the forest and elsewhere for purposes of war – at one time the lanes and roads on the outskirts of the village were stacked with bombs.[1]

The military presence in Oxford was soon very evident. Following the decision to double the size of the Territorial Army in March 1939, the 5th Battalion of the Oxfordshire and Buckinghamshire Light Infantry was reborn, taking recruits and later conscripts from North Oxfordshire while the 4th Battalion covered the southern part of the county. The 5th Battalion was stationed in Oxford at the beginning of the war with its headquarters in the premises of the University Air Squadron in St Cross Road. Within a month the battalion moved to North Oxfordshire, but the Regimental Depot at Cowley became an Infantry Training Centre housing about 1,500 men by the end of October 1939. Cowley Barracks was quite unequal to these numbers and a field between Brasenose Wood and Open Magdalen Wood was requisitioned as the site of Slade Camp, a hutted camp which was completed by March 1940. At the same time large areas of land on Shotover and at Horspath were acquired for military training.[2] As in the First World War, the Examination Schools were commandeered for use as a military hospital and, following a campaign by Professor Hugh Cairns, St Hugh's College opened as a hospital for head injuries in February 1940, dealing largely with injured despatch riders in its early days.[3]

After the outbreak of war, many other Oxfordshire towns and villages became used to accommodating Army units. The Headquarters Company of the 8th Battalion Durham Light Infantry was based at Charlbury and other soldiers from that regiment stayed at Kingham, commandeering the village's only petrol pump for military use. A contingent of the Royal Berkshire Regiment was also stationed at Charlbury for a time while guarding vulnerable places such as local

Cowley Barracks in February 1941. The Regimental Depot of the Oxfordshire and Buckinghamshire Light Infantry served as an Infantry Training Centre until American forces arrived in 1942.

aerodromes, Leafield Wireless Station and Blenheim Palace when it was occupied by the War Office.[4] A battalion of the Royal Fusiliers spent several months in Thame and men of the Royal Army Service Corps were based in Faringdon, leaving by train early one morning in January 1940:

> By this time, the sun was rising, turning the smoke from the engine to a cloud of gold. From the window of each compartment, the men waved and called to their friends who were now allowed on the platform. A last word, a last hand-clasp, and the train drew away into the mist, taking these men from us.[5]

In April the *Faringdon Advertiser* received a magazine from 'Somewhere in France' which included messages of appreciation to the townsfolk and these special greetings to some of Faringdon's young women:

> Doug sends his best love to Gwen
> Tom sends his best love to Florrie
> Horace sends his best love to Florrie
> Bill sends his best love to Florrie
> Dennis sends his best love to Vi
> Archie sends his best love to Edna
> Ronnie sends his best love to Winnie
> Jack sends his best love to Meg
> Ted sends his best love to Gert and Kath
> George sends his best love to Chriss
> Jack sends his best love to Nancy.[6]

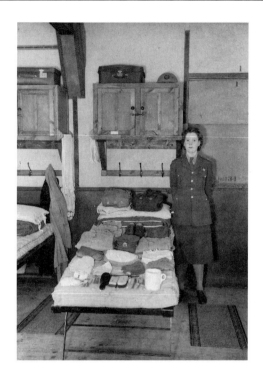

Kit inspection in Hut 34 at Slade Camp, Oxford, in July 1941. A woman in the Auxiliary Territorial Service (ATS) waits anxiously to see whether she has done enough to pass muster.

By the late 1930s the Royal Air Force had a substantial presence in Oxfordshire including updated First World War airfields at Bicester, Upper Heyford and Weston-on-the-Green, bomber stations at Abingdon, Benson and Harwell and a training school and maintenance unit at Brize Norton. On 2 September 1939, the departure of Fairey Battle bombers to join the Advanced Air Striking Force in France left a huge vacuum at most of the county's larger aerodromes which was filled almost at once by an important training role. Bicester was soon training pilots on Blenheim bombers, Harwell took two squadrons of Wellingtons and Upper Heyford trained crews for Hampden squadrons; Abingdon became an operational training centre for the striking force in France.[7] A less than respectful account of the training of two RAF observers appeared in the *Oxford Mail* in October 1939:

Before being taken up by a pilot officer for a flight over Oxford and neighbourhood they were informed that by means of charts, maps and instruments they were to work out the position of the plane and give instructions to the pilot.

After being in the air for about half an hour and poring over their maps, etc., they held an earnest conversation, at the end of which one of them said to the pilot, 'Excuse me, sir, would you mind removing your helmet?'

The pilot, greatly surprised, replied, 'Take my helmet off! Why?' Back came the answer, 'Well, sir, according to our calculations, the plane is now passing up the aisle of Christ Church Cathedral.'[8]

In November Berkshire County Council and racehorse trainers joined forces to protest at an Air Ministry scheme to use Odstone Down below White Horse Hill as a practice bombing range. The County Council Chairman, Ald. A.T. Loyd, commented:

> There is no need to explain to the Council how very sacred this particular part
> of Berkshire is. It is just below White Horse Hill, Wayland Smithy's cave, the
> Blowing Stone, all the very old pieces of Berkshire which we all cherish, and
> which are a matter of interest to visitors all over the country. We have to realize
> that the Air Ministry have powers to do anything they like. If they wish to take
> the land they can, but it is hardly fair to ask us to concur in the desecration of
> this particular part of the Berkshire Downs.

The Air Ministry held a demonstration of practice bombing on the proposed
range in April 1940 which proved that the bombs made no noise as they landed,
and the continued scepticism of representatives of the Racehorse Trainers
Association was not enough to defeat the scheme.[9]

The pace of activity suddenly became frenetic in May 1940 as the Germans
launched their Blitzkrieg against the Low Countries and neatly avoided 'France's
New Maginot Line', the subject of a confident but ill-timed article in the *Thame
Gazette*.[10] By the end of the month troops who had been evacuated from Dunkirk
were arriving in Oxford, among them members of the three battalions of the
Oxfordshire and Buckinghamshire Light Infantry which had been part of the British
Expeditionary Force. The *Oxford Mail* reported that the men were 'looking fit and
cheery', and asserted that most of the troops staying in Oxford had been driven to
their quarters.[11] Brian Mobley, however, recalled things differently:

> I remember the troops coming home and being marched to Cowley Barracks,
> that was a funny thing, I could never understand why it was that those chaps
> were made to march from Oxford station to Cowley Barracks absolutely
> exhausted and nobody laid on buses, I could never understand that. . . . We kids
> all sort of got round and carried their kitbags for them. . . . I well remember
> they all flopped down in Cowley Hospital grounds and said they weren't going
> any further until they'd had a rest. I suppose there were quite a lot of them and
> they eventually got off again but they . . . were half-dressed, half-naked,
> bandaged, wounded, a completely shocked, demoralized army at that time.[12]

Many of the soldiers were inevitably worn out by the time they reached
Cowley, but they were well looked after once they arrived:

> As the survivors poured in, so they were fed – no matter what the hour – and
> escorted to improvised accommodation. Men under training were squeezed
> into half the normal space, a camp was pitched in Brasenose Wood and men
> dossed down in the school and new gymnasium. Meanwhile, orderly room
> serjeants and their staff worked in shifts throughout the twenty-four hours
> recording arrivals. As soon as parties were collected they were sent to divisional
> concentration areas.

The arrivals became so numerous in early June that Major Jarvis and a band of
fifty men built a tented camp on Port Meadow which was occupied by the 131st

Soldiers who had been wounded at Dunkirk enjoy an outing to Bablockhythe while recuperating at Oxford's Radcliffe Infirmary in the summer of 1940.

Infantry Brigade. By 12 June 283 officers and 7,962 soldiers had made use of this accommodation or the facilities at Cowley, but it was claimed that training had never been interrupted. The chronicler of events for the Oxfordshire and Buckinghamshire Light Infantry reported that

> The full brunt fell on the cooks, who never took their boots off for a fortnight, and on Mr Jones and the officers' mess staff, who at any time of the day or night provided succulent meals for incoming officers.[13]

In this period of extreme crisis, thousands of troops and civilians were frantically busy constructing the GHQ Stop Lines which, in association with mobile forces, were intended to halt any German advance from beach-heads in south-east England. The Stop Line defences consisted of pill-boxes and anti-tank obstacles and extended east from Bristol to London and then northwards past the Wash to the North Sea coast near Middlesbrough. In the Oxford area the River Thames formed part of GHQ Stop Line (Red), and at Benson F.P. Chamberlain recalled the building of pill-boxes about half a mile apart in June and July 1940, mostly on the north bank of the river. One near his farm at Preston Crowmarsh was disguised as a summer-house and he estimated its cost at £500 or more; others were built to resemble hayricks.[14] At Long Wittenham an extensive tank trap took about 4½ acres off a riverside field at College Farm.[15] Running north from Oxford to Banbury, the Oxford Stop Line (Yellow) was envisaged as a barrier to east–west movement, although Southern Command was warned in August that

> about 37 accommodation bridges on the Oxford Canal will have to be left partially open for the benefit of farmers. It will take four men about one hour to do each bridge if they need to be blocked quickly.

The Stop Line scheme was the brainchild of General Ironside, but General Sir Alan Brooke, his successor as Commander-in-Chief, Home Forces from July 1940, soon declared his opposition to linear defence, preferring to station local mobile reserves near probable landing places. Within months, pill-boxes were discredited because 'they give a false sense of security to the garrison, make them static minded and prevent the full employment of their weapons'.[16]

At the same time, an English Resistance was being formed by Major Colin Gubbins with the improbable title of Auxiliary Units. Their hide-outs, stocked with arms and ammunition, food and fuel, were set back about 30 miles from the coast and extended from South Wales through southern and eastern England and up into Scotland. The units included men such as poachers, gamekeepers, farmers and mountaineers, who knew the countryside and would be able to live rough. At Coleshill House, near Faringdon, they were trained as a guerrilla army which would have carried out hit-and-run attacks to disrupt the progress of a German invasion.[17]

Many other precautions were taken during the summer of 1940 to deter aircraft from landing and to confuse the anticipated enemy parachutists. Potential landing grounds were identified in Oxford, and in July 1940 RAF Little Rissington agreed to take 'the necessary action in connection with the likelihood of Cutteslowe Park being used as a landing ground for enemy troops'. No special steps were thought necessary to prevent enemy landings on Hinksey Lake, but concrete posts were erected on Port Meadow and temporary stakes were used each night at Cowley airfield to deter airborne attacks. At Crowmarsh Battle Farm in Benson 500 large posts were put up in low-lying fields to prevent landings.[18] The manpower requirement for such tasks was awesome and the *Witney Gazette* included this urgent appeal:

DIGGERS WANTED

> Victory will be won, but the co-operation of all is essential. The Navy, the Army, and the Air Force are all doing their job. Here is one for you!
>
> The enemy will try all methods in his attempts to obtain a foothold in this Country and every obstacle must be placed in his way. The Air Force and the Army Authorities want your help to erect these obstacles.
>
> Your services, if offered now, may render some field unavailable to the enemy as a landing ground.
>
> As a British subject will you do your bit?[19]

Confusing the enemy; the removal of a road sign at the Woodstock Road roundabout to the north of Oxford.

Farmers were urged to obstruct all large fields 'with any kind of implements, carts, debris and timber' and were to place hayricks in the middle of fields not in the corner; a Buckland farmer was reported to be doing this in September[20].

The other contemporary strategy was to ensure that enemy troops would have to rely on their own resources in establishing where they were. Signposts were removed and milestones were defaced or, as in Oxford, covered with slabs of concrete.[21] Place-names on railway stations were removed although this regulation was relaxed in October 1940 to permit names that were under platform roofs and not visible from the road or from low-flying aircraft.[22] Farmers obliterated addresses on their farm carts, and in Benson the place-name was chipped off the war memorial. In June 1940 a correspondent to the *North Berks Herald* even suggested removing directories from telephone boxes because they might help newly arrived enemy troops to establish where they were.[23]

Between April 1939 and March 1940 the number of RAF aircraft based in Oxfordshire increased from 450 to about 1,250, and five Operational Training Units had been established. After Dunkirk, fear of air attacks on existing airfields led to the hurried building of satellite stations to which aircraft and personnel could be dispersed. These included Finmere (a satellite for Bicester and Upper Heyford), Mount Farm (serving Benson), and Stanton Harcourt (for Abingdon). RAF Weston-on-the-Green was the first Oxfordshire airfield to be bombed on 9 August, but a more serious attack on Stanton Harcourt, which was still under construction, and Brize Norton took place on the 16th.[24] The details were reported by the County's ARP Controller:

> At approximately 1745/16 3 enemy 'planes dived upon the run-way now under construction near Stanton Harcourt, dropped ten small bombs and directed machine-gun fire at civilian employees. . . . Casualties among the civilian personnel amounted to two men killed outright and 7 seriously wounded, 4 of whom have since died in hospital. These people, employees of the contractors, Wimpeys, had no chance to take cover, no warning having been received in the Area, the attack was sudden and unexpected. . . .

> At approximately 1756/16 2 enemy 'planes dropped bombs on the Brize Norton RAF Station. Reports indicate that 20 HE [High Explosive] and IB's [Incendiary Bombs] were dropped but the RAF has given no indication regarding the respective numbers of either. . . . Damage done on this occasion resulted in 2 hangars being burnt out, and a portion of Barrack building being partially demolished. The RAF called on Witney Sub-Control for all available ambulances and three were despatched, use being made of only 2. The Civilian casualties amounted to one killed and 3 injured. There were a number of wounded among the RAF personnel.[25]

Following this attack, aircraft from Brize Norton were dispersed to Akeman Street, a newly constructed Relief Landing Ground near Witney, and Southrop, and No. 15 Service Flying Training School left for Kidlington aerodrome on 19 August.[26]

Tension was high and there was panic in Charlbury one night when the church bells rang at 2 a.m., but this invasion signal turned out to have been given by a deserter.[27] On 1 July Local Defence Volunteers were alerted by an urgent Police Priority Enemy Report:

> Sgt. Jones of Field Security 1st Canadian Division no fixed station reports that approximately 1815 hrs. to-day 2 parachutists dropped from an aeroplane, believed to be German, in proximity of Nettlebed one has been arrested who was in possession of pedal cycle, it is believed that the person not arrested has two identity cards, one in the name of Henry Evans and the other of Albert Williams, wearing grey flannel suit, no hat, age 32, fair, speaks English. Stop.

The arrested man had particulars and a map of Manor Farm at Hardwick near Witney and stated that he and his companion had instructions to meet Mr J.E. Florey who would supply them with explosives for sabotage. He was taken back to Canadian Military Headquarters at Shotover House and troops descended on Hardwick, ransacking the farmhouse for incriminating documents and arresting Mr Florey and his family on the suspicion of being Fifth Columnists. Prolonged interrogation, however, exposed the 'German parachutist' as a deserter from a searchlight regiment at Hereford who had invented the whole story because he had worked for Mr Florey and had a grudge against him.[28]

On 7 September 1940 there was a further scare when Southern Command was convinced that invasion had started and church bells were rung:

Charlbury was the most northerly place in which this alarm was sounded. . . . A Red Cross worker described how she woke with a start and shouted to her husband (a very tired warden), 'Invasion!' As he turned over sleepily he replied, 'It's a change from the siren anyway.'[29]

In an atmosphere of crisis it was hardly surprising that deep suspicion fell upon those people whose loyalty and commitment could be questioned. Foreigners were a particular source of anxiety and when Herman Solf, a German graduate student living on Boars Hill, made the mistake of filming a crashed RAF plane in February 1940, the case aroused a national furore about aliens. Imprisoned for one month for an infringement of Defence Regulations, Solf was subsequently interned and then deported, surviving the sinking of his first ship to languish for the rest of the war in Australia.[30] In Oxford there was heightened concern about the large number of aliens living locally, and German-born Dr Eva Glees recalled that foreign nationals had to appear before a tribunal where they were classified as Grade A, Nazis or Nazi sympathizers; Grade B, Doubtful Aliens; or Grade C, Genuine Aliens. The Government bowed to pressure at the end of May and decided to intern all enemy aliens; Oxford's Chief Constable, C.R. Fox, reported in June that this action would be popular and, within a month, 143 aliens living in the city had been transferred to internment camps. The scare was not over, however, since almost 1,800 aliens were among the refugees who poured into Oxford as evacuees during the autumn of 1940. Dr Glees' husband was one of only three German men in Oxford who escaped internment,[31] and H.W.B. Joseph's diary shows that, in May 1941, a German woman could even arouse suspicion by taking a walk in the country:

> I was told that A.P. Poynton a few days' since noticed a young woman at Islip moving about a field with a map who hastily put it away when he approached. He rang up the police and she was very soon apprehended, and found to be a German student at one of the women's colleges – and interned.[32]

The principled stand of conscientious objectors, or 'conchies' as they were derisively termed, stirred up understandably bitter feelings in a nation that was fighting for its very survival. An editorial in the *Witney Gazette* in May 1940 argued that

> the majority of objectors want simply to escape a nasty job of work, while desiring to live in that security which others are willing to shed their blood to preserve.[33]

In some areas local authorities cut the wages of conscientious objectors among their employees to match those of privates in the army; in July 1940 Oxford City Council considered, but did not adopt, a proposal to sack 'These yellow-blooded men'.[34] Some men bowed to the moral pressure, but a significant number pursued their claim to special tribunals where they argued, usually on religious grounds, that they should be exempt from military service. Teachers formed the largest occupational group at local tribunals, but the best-known individual was undoubtedly John Stafford Cripps, the son of Sir Stafford Cripps, who argued that 'to take part in the war machine was . . . contrary to the spirit of Christian teaching'; in his case, the tribunal ruled that his work as a journalist was of sufficient importance. Many objectors were registered for non-combatant service, particularly in the Royal Army Medical Corps, or for work of national importance such as horticultural, agricultural or land drainage work.[35]

As the war progressed, the armed forces continued to extend their presence across much of Oxfordshire. Michael Bowyer has identified twenty-seven wartime airfields in the county and the later ones included relief landing grounds such as those at Barford St John, Chipping Norton, Kingston Bagpuize and Kiddington, and satellite airfields like Edgehill and Enstone. At Watchfield and its satellite at Kelmscott pilots were trained in blind approach flying, which became more important because of the increase in night flying. In late 1941 Shellingford became the home of the much-travelled No. 3 Elementary Flying Training School. After the United States entered the war, airfields at Grove, Mount Farm and Chalgrove were taken over by the United States Army Air Force (USAAF). Four hundred Americans arrived at Chalgrove by lorry from Culham station in the early morning of 9 January 1944:

> They seemed to delight in moving in great convoys, unable to resist the allure of night life except for military operations! . . . Another curious habit they displayed was delight in leaning out of lorry cabs, as foreigners lean out of trains. It made the passage of American vehicles extremely hazardous for hapless cyclists who, whether they liked it or not, frequently became recipients of chewed (or unchewed) gum.[36]

A decoy airfield was built at Golder Manor to confuse the enemy,[37] but almost equally improbable in land-locked Oxfordshire was HMS *Hornbill* at Culham, an Aircraft Receipt and Despatch Unit for the Royal Navy Air Service which was commissioned on 1 November 1944.[38]

In 1941 Benson airfield was enlarged to take four-engined bombers, causing the destruction of several houses and requiring the closure and partial re-routing of the main Oxford–Henley road. A phlegmatic local inhabitant confessed that 'It shocked us a little . . .'.[39] The building of an RAF Maintenance Unit in the beechwoods near Woodcote was similarly disruptive:

> Its beginnings in 1941 were very noisy. The blasting of trees in the woods shook our homes. Lorries loaded with sand, gravel, steel and corrugated iron roared through the village. Then gradually the monstrous black huts reared their heads.[40]

RAF Eynsham, built to the south-west of the village in 1941, was one of a chain of Air Ammunition Parks receiving supplies of high explosives from major underground storage sites for forward transmission to local bomber airfields. Its initial capacity was 1,000 tons but this was later raised to 6,000 tons, and from September 1943 satellite storage facilities were provided beside the estate roads in Eynsham Hall Park.[41]

The proliferation of airfields was so great that Oxfordshire was said to have more to the square mile than any other part of the British Isles, and there never seemed a time by day or by night when there were not planes in the air; trainer-planes, isolated German planes who more than once nipped in and caused havoc before their presence was known, our planes going out to Germany, enemy planes on their way to the industrial Midlands, and to South Wales.[42]

Sporadic raids on local airfields continued into 1941 with RAF Benson being attacked on 30 January and 27 February, and Abingdon suffering considerable damage from two bombing raids in March. On 12 August an enemy plane chanced upon Airspeed Oxfords on a night-flying exercise from Weston-on-the-Green and shot one down near Sturdy's Castle, killing both members of the crew. The raider then dropped six bombs on the airfield, damaging seven planes before making his escape. These intruders were not always so fortunate and, on 13 November 1940, a Junkers Ju88 bomber crashed near Blewbury, responsibility being claimed by Spitfires of 611 Squadron and by Lewis gunners at RAF Bicester; one crew member died and was buried at Harwell while his three colleagues were taken prisoner.[43] Since enemy incursions into Oxfordshire were comparatively rare, the dog fights regularly seen in the south-east were uncommon in this area, but Mrs Warner remembered one near Ascott-under-Wychwood as she and Miss Cox returned from a funeral procession:

we just reached our house when there came such a banging and a booming. she says 'Coo Thunder' and popped her head under my coat only to pop out again say[ing] 'no it aint Its only them blooming Germans!' Then she scrambled up the bank and yelled 'Look at them fighting Go it lads Get him' then all the solemn procession climbed up the bank to see the dog fight of planes over the Radio Station about three miles away. all yelling and cheering as they brought him down. It seemed a strange end to a funeral.[44]

The sheer number of flights over Oxfordshire, many of them by trainee bomber and glider pilots, made a series of accidents almost inevitable. At Upper Heyford, for example, two Hampden bombers collided when barely airborne on 13 August 1940. Two planes from Harwell were lost in separate accidents in August 1942; on the 21st a Wellington returning from a night flight collided with an Oxford over Chipping Norton and both planes crashed on to the town in flames. Just four nights later, two Wellingtons, one from Harwell and one from Hampstead Norris, collided over Odstone bombing range and the Harwell plane came down near Uffington. The training of glider pilots in Oxfordshire began early in 1942 and led to further accidents such as the one on 2 September 1942 when a plane towing a Hotspur glider crashed into the steeple of St Mary's Church at Witney; miraculously, the occupants of the plane survived and nobody on the ground was injured.[45]

Not all the accidents involved aircraft in training; in the early hours of 20 May 1944, for example, a Lancaster bomber returning from a raid in Europe was diverted to RAF Benson because of fog and crashed into a barn at Crowmarsh Battle Farm, killing three men out of the crew of seven.[46] In Wallingford a major disaster was averted in the same year when two crewmen of the Royal Canadian Air Force lost their lives after they refused to bale out of their crippled, bomb-laden aircraft and crash-landed it clear of the town; they were later commemorated by the local street names, Andrew Road and Wilding Road.[47]

Few bombing raids were launched from Oxfordshire although local Operational Training Units did provide substantial numbers of aircraft for the large-scale raids on Cologne, Essen and Bremen in May and June 1942; more typically, bomber crews flew propaganda leaflet missions over Occupied France as part of their final training. RAF Bicester and Harwell also had an important role in delivering aircraft to Gibraltar or over France to Malta and Egypt.[48] Benson became the home of No. 1 Photographic Reconnaissance Unit in December 1940 and its Spitfires and Mosquitoes were soon flying missions throughout Europe to photograph strategic sites and record the effects of Allied bombing.[49] One such mission was recalled by Flying Officer Gerald Fray:

> It was a warm summer day, August 9th 1943 to be precise, and I was detailed in the morning for a 'job' in Southern France. The weather was perfect, with hardly a cloud in the sky. All went well until the return journey, when I developed engine trouble. After two anxious hours I just managed to reach the South Coast, where I landed and was picked up by another aircraft and brought back to base.
>
> As I cycled home to the farm, around 4.0 pm, I stopped by the Dollar Turn. It was Harvest time – a Lister engine chugging at a loaded elevator – dusty men and girls busy ricking – others 'stooking' – and someone gleaning. Then I realised that four hours before I had been over 500 miles away, with 300 miles of Occupied France and the Channel between me and Benson. How peaceful it all was after the ceaseless roar of engine, the dry rubbish smell of oxygen and mask.[50]

To peaceful Benson came the first pictures of the breached Mohne and Sorpe Dams in 1943 and views of Peenemunde where the Germans were developing the V1 and V2 weapons. Members of the Women's Auxiliary Air Force working as Photograph Interpreters at the requisitioned Old Mansion at Ewelme helped to identify the V1 launch sites so early that Allied raids were able to delay the first use of these weapons. The United States Army Air Force began flying photographic reconnaissance missions from Mount Farm in February 1943 and from Chalgrove a year later. Their main purpose was to record enemy forces and strategic sites in France in preparation for D-Day, but later flights photographed V1 launch sites and provided advance information for the airborne attack on Arnhem and the Battle of the Bulge.[51]

Much of the military training and preparation in wartime Oxfordshire achieved its purpose when the Allied forces established a successful beach-head in Normandy in June 1944. The county had in fact become a vast storehouse of arms and equipment which included the enlarged Central Ordnance Depot at Didcot and another massive Ordnance Depot at Arncott near Bicester which was built in 1941–2. The latter has been described as 'the largest single military project ever launched in the United Kingdom' and, with an estimated cost of £6.5 million, it provided 6,739,000 sq ft of covered storage, 5,177,000 sq ft of open storage and required 47½ miles of railway and about 24 miles of new roads. At the beginning of 1942 about 1,500 Royal Engineers, 607 men from the Pioneer

The building of the Central Ordnance Depot near Bicester in 1942, photographed from a Spitfire. Lower Arncott (left) and Upper Arncott (middle right) are entangled within a bewildering complex of new railways, roads and Nissen huts.

Corps and 550 Italian prisoners of war were working on the site, and their numbers were later augmented by further companies of the Pioneer Corps and the 3rd Non Combatant Corps. When completed, the Depot housed 7,671 military personnel in Nissen hutted barracks, including soldiers in the Royal Army Ordnance Corps and up to 4,000 women in the Auxiliary Territorial Service. Vehicles, ordnance and other supplies poured in during 1943 and huge amounts of stores were shipped out to support the Normandy landings and later operations.[52] On 15 December 1941 the 22nd Vehicle Reserve Depot, one of the largest in England, was set up among the trees in Cornbury Park and, within four weeks, consisted of 3,000 jeeps, ambulances and other army vehicles. In a secluded part of Wychwood Forest at least a mile from any house a large consignment of high explosives was stored prior to D-Day, being transported and packed by black American soldiers.[53] E.J. Lainchbury recalled that, by 1944, hundreds of thousands of shells and bombs were stored on roadside verges for miles around Kingham.

Bombs stacked by the roadside between Eynsham and Freeland early in 1944. Stockpiles like this became a familiar sight in Oxfordshire in the months leading up to D-Day.

When necessary, all this material had to be transported to the south coast as quickly as possible and, during 1942 and 1943, Kingham station on the main line between Oxford and Worcester was provided with a seven-track siding and a railway yard to speed the loading and unloading of trucks.[54] New sidings were created at Yarnton Junction and at Moreton Cutting near Didcot, and the extensive Hinksey marshalling yards were built at Oxford in 1942. The most significant railway improvement, however, was the double-tracking of much of the Didcot, Newbury and Southampton railway which took eight months from August 1942 to April 1943 and enabled some 16,000 military trains to use the route in the year leading up to D-Day.[55]

Military manoeuvres became a regular sight, and after tank exercises in Ewelme 'Odd corners of our street were sliced off, a few walls pushed over, and deep chewed gashes in the grass showed where they had rested'.[56] Many windows were smashed during the Battle of Oxford at the end of January 1943, and in North Oxford an escaping tank destroyed one of the notorious Cutteslowe Walls. One theory was that the driver was a disgruntled man from the council houses beyond the private housing estate. Much of the action arising from the ambitious Exercise Spartan in March 1943 took place in the Oxford area where British and Canadian troops advancing from 'Southland' met troops of Eastern Command representing German 'Eastland'. Royal Engineers from the Bailey Bridge training camp at Howbery Park near Wallingford were able to test their skills at

An ignominious end for a Sherman tank which crashed through the parapet of Burford Bridge during an exercise and fell into the River Windrush.

Shillingford and Osney, and Bren gun carriers passed in convoy along Beaumont Street. A special newspaper was published by the *Oxford Mail* for troops in the field, local delivery being made by a pony and trap hired from a Kidlington farmer.[57] As D-Day approached, Burford was made very much aware of the American forces stationed nearby:

> The 600-year-old bridge, which carries the north–south route through the town, resounded to the continual passing of tanks and other mechanical monsters. It is a bare 15 feet between parapets and winds considerably, so that when a group of four bulldozing machines, each 70 feet long and something like 12 feet wide, came to cross, they were watched with interest. The first just cleared, the second went right down the middle with excellent judgement, the third only just got over without scraping and the fourth had to be manhandled clear, leaving its heavy mark upon the western parapet.
>
> On another occasion the eastern parapet was almost entirely destroyed by a Sherman tank which, when going northwards, lost a track on the southern approach and, before it could be stopped, went over the side and remained with its nose in the mud of the river and its tail on the roadway. After pushing and pulling without success for a day or so, it was eventually towed along the bed of the river, and hauled up the bank into Dr Cheatle's garden.[58]

For the RAF, final preparations included the construction of an airfield at Broadwell which opened on 15 November 1943. This new station was to deliver airborne forces and supplies, undertake transport runs to the Continent after a bridgehead had been established and bring wounded troops back from the battlefront. Nearby on the Bradwell Grove estate a military hospital was built, which was taken over in the spring of 1944 by the US Army to become the 61st General Hospital with 1,500 beds and a total population of over 2,000.[59] The Americans also set up the 317th General Hospital on Ramsden Heath[60] and took over the Churchill in Oxford, a War Emergency Medical Service hospital which became the 91st General Hospital. The latter provided 600 beds in its original brick buildings, 600 more in Nissen huts and a further 400 in tent-type wards and other huts. Facilities were described in some detail when Queen Elizabeth paid a visit in July 1944 and was shown round by Colonel L.M. Dyke, Commanding Officer of the hospital, and the Chief Nurse, Captain Frances Kasmark. She was taken to

> the operating theatre, to the kitchens, to the admirably appointed recreation room, which has fine views, and she took tea with the nursing staff in the officers' and nurses' mess hall. She also visited the eye, ear, nose and throat department.
>
> The Queen was particularly interested in the hospital's cleverly designed extension. It consists of a series of brown marquees, each standing on a cement base. The lighting in these tents, which are in the centre of a grass quadrangle, is almost as excellent as in the wards themselves.[61]

In early March 1944 Harwell closed as an Operational Training Unit and it reopened on 1 April as part of 38 Group, Airborne Forces; with Broadwell, it was to play a vital role in the D-Day landings and later airborne assaults. Intensive training exercises took place from both airfields in May and June, and RAF Kelmscott was used as a dropping zone for Polish paratroops during May. A local man recalled:

> The sky was black with Dakotas and then hundreds of 'chutes appeared in the sky. Many soldiers missed the airfield dropping zone completely, and landed in fields and trees for miles around – you always knew when they were jumping as the ambulances arrived before the planes!

One drop did in fact have fatal consequences when a plane came in too low and four men from the 1st Polish Parachute Brigade were killed.[62] By the beginning of June, however, preparations were complete and, on the 5th, Benson residents noticed that dispersed aircraft at the airfield had suddenly sported distinctive white stripes.[63] With a favourable weather forecast that evening, the invasion of Normandy was given the green light and first to leave from Tarrant Rushton in Wiltshire was a glider-borne task force from the 52nd Light Infantry led by former Oxford City policeman, Major John Howard. The Oxfordshire and Buckinghamshire Light Infantry therefore provided the first fighting troops to land in Europe and their primary task, before the arrival of the main paratroop force, was to capture intact two crucial bridges, one over the River Orne at

*Major John Howard leads the 2nd Battalion, Oxfordshire and Buckinghamshire Light
Infantry during a Salute the Soldier Week parade in St Giles', Oxford, in May 1944. A few
weeks later, he was spearheading the Normandy invasion.*

Ranville and the other at Benouville crossing the Caen Canal. The operation went
almost perfectly with three gliders landing beside each bridge and the defenders
being overpowered before they could destroy the structures. The Benouville
bridge has since been known as Pegasus Bridge after the divisional insignia worn
by the attacking force:

> Certain moments are vivid in the minds of those who fought by the canal and
> the river from before dawn till after dusk on that long summer day. There was
> the sound of Major Howard's victory signal travelling over the night wind to
> the ears of the parachutists struggling to reach and reinforce the bridge. There
> was the large hole which gaped in the side of the water tower at Benouville,
> hiding a nest of snipers. It had been punched by the first shot fired by a
> captured German anti-tank gun. There was Monsieur Gondree in the little
> café by the bridge, tending the wounded and adding to the noise of battle a
> more convivial sound. He uncorked ninety-seven bottles of champagne,
> carefully hidden for just such a day as that (the German occupying force had
> been kept happy with a concoction made by his wife of rotting melons and half-
> fermenting sugar, which they bought at twenty-five francs the glass and drank

with avidity). . . . There were the red berets of General Gale and Brigadier Poett as they walked across the bridges at about ten in the morning, 'for all the world like umpires at an exercise'. There were the gliders 'swaying and rustling' through the evening air, bringing reinforcements and supplies.[64]

At 11 p.m. on the evening of 5 June six Albemarles took off from RAF Harwell to spearhead Operation Tonga. Each plane dropped ten men to set up beacons to guide the main paratroop force which left soon afterwards. The first aircraft from Broadwell was airborne at 11.14 p.m. and the Dakotas of 512 and 575 Squadrons dropped 952 paratroops on to French soil in the early hours of 6 June.[65] An early riser recorded that

> the most awe-inspiring sight in Charlbury during the war was on D-Day, when fleets of gliders came over in the very early morning. The sun had risen and the sky was red; the gliders, with this background, made a very beautiful and inspiring picture.[66]

Aircraft from Broadwell and Harwell took further reinforcements to Normandy as part of Operation Mallard during the afternoon of 6 June. The rest of the men from the 52nd Light Infantry were carried in gliders from Harwell as Major J. Granville recorded:

> An impressive array of Horsa gliders lined up on the edge of the runway awaited us. A brief command and we split up into our glider parties and waited for the order to emplane. The impression that I got was that the men were quiet, but confident and keen to get on with the job. Such laughter as there was seemed slightly forced and directed mainly at remarks, some rude, some humorous, chalked on the fuselages of the gliders. At about 1830 hours, with final wishes of bon voyage over, we were in our gliders. In the glider we all wore Mae Wests and had a rapid rehearsal of our ditching drill in case we 'pranged' in the English Channel. Then with safety belts adjusted we waited for the jerk as the tug took the strain on the tow rope. Soon it came and those in the front seats could see themselves hurtling down the runway behind the tug. Then we were airborne and once again we heard the familiar whistle as the air rushed by and we glided higher and higher into the evening air.[67]

In the weeks that followed, Harwell took part in supply drops for Special Operations Executive. Dakotas from Broadwell began to retrieve battlefield casualties from France on 17 June and this formed a major task until the ill-fated attempt to seize the Rhine crossing at Arnhem was launched on 17 September, and in the Benson area 'our sky was literally full of aircraft towing gliders'. Broadwell's contribution on that day was to deliver 41 gliders carrying 544 troops and equipment to a landing zone west of Arnhem. Stirlings from Harwell also carried glider-borne troops on the 17th and suffered a number of losses in later attempts to re-supply the increasingly desperate Allied forces. The depleted Harwell squadrons were soon transferred to Essex, but Broadwell resumed its role of carrying supplies to the Continent and returning with casualties.[68]

As the tide of war changed in the Allies' favour, prisoners of war began to be housed in the county. A camp for Italian prisoners of war was opened in Harcourt Hill, North Hinksey, in 1942 and hundreds of others were accommodated at the Windmill Camp below Blackthorn Hill; when they were not helping to build the Ordnance Depot, the prisoners at Blackthorn whiled away their leisure hours by creating several impressive sculptures which survived for years in what became a scrapyard.[69] At Didcot an army camp was converted into a prisoner of war camp after Allied troops had moved out, and Mario Corradi recalled that Italians arriving at Byfield in 1944 'had to make a camp, a POW camp ourself . . . lot of nice building . . . then they shut the gate and you were in'.[70] The Italians were extensively used as labourers and a booklet, *Pidgin English for Italian Prisoners of War*, was published for 'selected . . . prisoners . . . to assist in overcoming the shortage of interpreters required for working parties'.[71] After D-Day, German prisoners of war arrived and Willi Skoda was sent to the North Hinksey camp in 1945, going out with a working party to build an agricultural camp in Witney and then undertaking farmwork in Woodeaton. By this time, security at the camp was perhaps running down and he recalled:

Well, first of all, I was surprised. Not many guards, the fence was easy to get out of. Then, I think once some got out but didn't try to run away because there was no point, they just pick the flowers.[72]

Apart from the physical effects of the new airfields, camps and other installations, the huge military presence in Oxfordshire had wide-ranging consequences. There were, for example, thousands of men and women to house and although many were accommodated in huts and temporary camps, others had to be billeted on local people as Doris Chamberlain at Benson remembered:

We had a full house from Spring 1940 when a very nice Scotch Lt. in the REs [Royal Engineers] came knocking on the door asking if we could put up his wife and small daughter. It was the first time we had contemplated having billetees and it took a little arranging and fixing. However, since then we took in a long succesion partly because the police called one day and enquired how many rooms we had and we were told we must accomodate 12 people. Some stayed only a few weeks before being posted and others were with us for 3 years or more. We had REs, RAF, civilians, some with wives and then later 4 Landgirls.[73]

Many properties were required for military accommodation and, before a system of requisitioning had been properly instituted, it was a case of 'get what you can'. Thus, when the 5th Battalion, Oxfordshire and Buckinghamshire Light Infantry was moved out of Oxford in October 1939,

Local knowledge proved useful, and we got Wykham Park easily, Red House, Bodicote, with some difficulty, and 'Greenhill,' Adderbury, with great exertion, the owner going so far as to try to bribe [Lieutenant-Colonel] Bertram Long.[74]

There was quite a battle for Thornbury House at Kidlington when the RAF and the Red Cross were beaten off by the boarders of East Ham Grammar School for Girls. The Clerk to Oxfordshire County Council confessed in November 1940 that

Owing to the extreme shortage of any sort of accommodation in this district there has been, up to this moment, a most unfortunate scramble for any empty house and it has often been a matter of the house falling to the person who gets there first.[75]

There was a similar fight for Bignell House where the BBC tried unsuccessfully to dislodge the RAF and Oxfordshire County Council in February 1941. Unoccupied at the outbreak of the war, this large Victorian mansion was uneasily shared between personnel from RAF Bicester, the Bignell Park Evacuated School and the owners, Mr and Mrs Payne, who had presumably returned to try to safeguard their property. By their presence they were able to prevent the sort of mayhem that occurred at Basildon House when troops lit a fire on the floor of an upstairs bedroom, but their situation was distinctly unenviable. In July 1941, for instance, they persuaded the Clerk to the County Council to make this complaint to the Group Captain, RAF Bicester:

It has been reported to me that members of the personnel from your Station occupying the top rooms of the above-named premises, have been out on the leads and by jumping from one level to another has [sic] brought away a portion of the roof, causing water to pour in to Mr and Mrs Payne's flat and so doing damage. It will be a great convenience if the exploration of the leads by your men can now be definitely put 'out of bounds'.

It is unclear whether this letter had any effect, but a schedule of damage the following January included cigarette burns on the floors and furniture, a broken piano pedal, a knocked over and chipped urn on the terrace and lino damaged by the acid from a fire appliance.[76]

Massively increased traffic levels were another consequence of local military activity. In Philip Larkin's novel *Jill*, which is set in wartime Oxford, John Kemp is aware of 'hooded Army lorries thundering past at eight-second intervals'. Along the main roads near Wootton,

the convoys rolled and rumbled endlessly by day and by night, and we saw some strange cargoes, vast unfamiliar machinery, 'ducks', crashed aeroplanes. There were jeeps and tanks, and lorries and armoured cars, with fancy feminine names lightheartedly chalked across them.[77]

Military traffic signs appeared everywhere, even in the heart of Oxford, and in the Burford area residents noted 'the mysterious "70", black on a circular yellow ground, which was . . . discovered later to indicate a bridge or culvert which could carry the heaviest tanks'.[78]

For a child in Eynsham the constant bustle was the source of many memories:

Excitement came when a convoy came down our road. To avoid the toll gate bridge the tanks and other vehicles would come along the A40, along

American military signs adorn a pedestrian refuge at the Carfax end of High Street, Oxford, c. 1944.

Cassington Road, turn up Queen Street into High Street and then into Station Road. All the 'war' traffic therefore had to pass our house. We would hear the shout 'Spatchie coming', which meant a dispatch rider was heading for the corner to direct the coming convoy in Queen Street. We would all run out to see the fun and shout 'Any gum, chum?' to the soldiers. If it was very cold my mother or one of the neighbours would make a bucket of cocoa and the vehicles would slow down so that the men could dip their cups in for a drink on their way through. Once my sister, who was only two years old at the time, was on the far side of the road when the tanks started coming round the corner. My terrified mother just shouted and shouted for her to stand still. It was a great relief when the convoy ended and mother could retrieve her.

Not everyone was so fortunate of course and in July 1942 a six-year-old Eynsham girl was run over and killed by an RAF articulated lorry; in March 1945 an Eynsham man aged seventy-one was knocked down by a US ambulance that was said to have been travelling at between 50 and 60 miles an hour.[79] New hazards faced all road users and in May 1944, for example, the regular bus from Watlington to Reading collided with a tank near Assendon although no one was hurt in the accident.[80] At Bicester the amount of traffic generated by nearby camps led to the introduction of a one-way traffic scheme in the town centre in December 1943.[81]

Military training sometimes left behind real danger for the unwary and this was tragically demonstrated at Banbury in August 1943 when two boys aged eight and twelve were killed after a live mortar bomb had been found on a practice bombing range. Eleven-year-old Jackie Smirthwaite recalled that he and a friend had gone blackberrying on Monday afternoon:

We took with us our little 'buggy' (a home-made wooden plank-truck on wheels) and passing what all we boys call the 'Amma-biff' Alan asked me if I would like to get some shrapnel. I said yes, and we went together into a nearby field. We had not been there for a very long time previous to this. Directly we got past the gate we saw a lot of pieces of shrapnel lying on the ground, but we did not touch them. We then went over to where the little grassy hills are and there saw lots more pieces of exploded ammunition. Lying on the top of the ground, not buried in any way, was a strange looking object like a thick handle of a cricket bat. It was covered in dirt on the outside, and Alan said, 'Let's take it home and show our mum.'

The children carried the mortar bomb back to their homes, fighting off an older boy who wanted to add it to his collection, but it exploded in the street the same evening.[82]

Increased crime was blamed on military personnel, and in July 1940 the Chief Constable of Oxford blamed the temporary presence of Canadian troops in the city for a marked increase in the theft of bicycles, the 'borrowing' of cars and drunkenness. In September 1943 two soldiers from the King's Royal Rifle Corps were fined in Bicester for stealing the bikes of two aircraftswomen in the WAAF.[83]

After the United States entered the war at the end of 1941, the arrival of large numbers of American personnel was welcomed by many people but not by everyone. The virtual segregation of the American armed forces aroused some

Six United States airmen pose for the camera at Packer's Studio in Chipping Norton, c. 1943.

hostility since local people were appalled that black soldiers had been 'trained to step into the gutter when passing "White Folk" in the streets' and the Americans could not understand why the British accepted blacks as equals.[84] The Allies also found that they were divided, rather than united, by a common language and the United States War and Navy Departments issued newly arrived American troops with *A Short Guide to Great Britain*, which included this helpful advice:

It isn't a good idea, for instance, to say 'bloody' in mixed company in Britain – it is one of their worst swear words. To say: 'I look like a bum' is offensive to their ears, for to the British this means that you look like your own backside. . . . Don't be misled by the British tendency to be soft-spoken and polite. If they need to be, they can be plenty tough. The English language didn't spread across the oceans and over the mountains and jungles and swamps of the world because these people were panty-waists.

The guide ended with a glossary of useful terms and these few examples indicate the rich potential for confusion or embarrassment:

automobile – motor car, or car
bathrobe – dressing gown
bill – banknote, or note
candy (hard) – boiled sweets
conductor – guard
cookie – biscuit
deck (of cards) – pack
drawers (men's) – pants
freight car – goods wagon
garters (men's) – sock suspenders
gasoline, or gas – petrol
guy – bloke, fellow
highball – whiskey and soda
junk – rubbish
movie house – cinema
okay – righto
rubbers – galoshes
run (in a stocking) – ladder
suspenders (men's) – braces
ten pins – nine pins
trolley – tram
vest – waistcoat
'you're connected' – 'you're through' (telephone)[85]

In November 1943 Major David Moore, a doctor with the US Army Medical Corps, spoke to the Banbury Rotary Club and praised the way that American troops had been received. At the same time,

He appealed for tolerance in cases where American troops had acted with indiscretion, saying that there was a danger of a false impression created by

Passing the Bridge of Sighs; American servicemen are shown round the heart of Oxford by volunteer guides.

men who were out of their native environment. He spoke of the danger also of deriving their impression of America from the films of Hollywood, and the American novels. America, he pointed out, was not just one thing any more than England was one thing. Generally speaking, the infiltration of American troops into this country had been accomplished with comparatively little disturbance. The American soldier, for the most part, liked the English and got along with them well. . . . 'We feel we are exactly the same as you people,' he said, 'except that we went away across the ocean and have now come back. We feel at home although we have never been here before. There are a good many Americans here to-day who are very glad to be here and very glad to see the people and we only hope that when we go back you won't be entirely sorry that we came.'[86]

In Oxford men and women from a local RAF unit and American military hospital staff met socially from the middle of 1942, but the idea of a 'Fraternity

Dinner' such as the one they shared at the Angel Café in January 1944 was unusual enough to attract comment.[87] In general, British and American troops tended not to fraternize and there was real dismay at Cowley in 1942 when it was learned that the Infantry Training Centre was to be moved to Colchester and American forces were to be billeted in the barracks:

> This is a major blow to the Regiment. No date or destination has been given, but I am to be allowed to leave two officers and six men behind to look after our interests. I dare not leave the Regimental Museum where it is because our allies from experience are adept in scrounging and a souvenir to them is more than a memento. I am therefore trying to find a home for all the contents en bloc down in Oxford. Even if I could bar the present windows, which I can't, I should not feel happy leaving the museum to the tender mercies of alien cracksmen.[88]

Wherever they went, the better paid, more smartly dressed Americans attracted the envious comment that they were 'Over-paid, Over-sexed and Over here'. Bored with the lack of entertainment in one country village, some Americans hired their own club-room with a radiogram where 'every taste is catered for, for the sedate waltzer to the hottest of the "swing" enthusiast'.[89] At the instigation of the WVS Centre Organizer in Charlbury, a Welcome Club for the Americans based at Ramsden Heath was held weekly in Mr Hughes' billiard room from 1 February 1944:

> Tea, coffee and cakes were provided, games were obtained through a Government organisation and occasionally special features, such as competitions, were arranged. The piano was very popular. At one time a slight hitch arose through the Americans seeing the girls home with too much fervour; one of them explained that he 'figured it out that a girl would be kind of insulted if you saw her home and did not offer to kiss her'![90]

Many local women were swept off their feet by the easygoing charm of the Americans and in March 1944 the *Oxford Mail* announced the first 'Anglo-American wedding' in Chipping Norton between Rose Watson and Corporal Philip Brown of the US Army who came from Pittsburgh.[91] Elsie Gibbs of Fritwell was another of the local GI brides, marrying Sergeant Leslie Ferrell from West Virginia in August 1945.[92] The Americans also appealed to youngsters like George Crook because they tended to be fond of children, gave out sweets and had more patience than most British adults.[93]

Throughout the war, Oxford was seen as a place where troops could enjoy rest and recreation. In April 1940 the English Speaking Union established a free social club for women in uniform at No. 3 Cornmarket Street, and just two months later the YMCA converted the Carfax Assembly Rooms opposite into a forces' canteen with reading and writing rooms and facilities for indoor games.[94] Later, the nearby Clarendon Hotel, reprieved by the war from demolition for a new Woolworth's, became the American Red Cross Club.[95] Members of the armed forces in uniform were allowed free admittance to the Bodleian Library and the English Speaking Union organized educational hospitality programmes for American servicemen who stayed in colleges and were treated to lectures,

One of Oxfordshire's GI brides; wedding group outside Littlemore parish church in May 1945 after the marriage of Edna McCluskey and Robert Clark.

discussion groups, guided tours of the city, a dance at Rhodes House and a tea-party with Lady Tweedsmuir.[96] Overseas troops were sometimes given an official welcome and on 12 April 1940, for instance, the Mayor of Oxford entertained a party of about 200 Canadians at the Town Hall. In the same year the mayor was given a rather different role by a lonely driver stationed with the Royal Army Service Corps at Bampton:

Dear Sir

I know it is a cheek to write to you but I though I would try my luck. I have no gril fraind so wonder if you could find me one I am 21 yrs old and would like a gril frind about 19 to 20 yrs old and I was a Chauffur before the War I am not bad to look at but am very shy. I should also like a gril not bad looking with dark hair some one to have not for past time but for keeps please find me some one because it very lonly down here and I am a long way from home.

Yours Turly
Drv. W. Hird
No. 139639

Thanking you so much.[97]

Many off-duty servicemen would have visited Oxford with a similar motive although most were probably content to forget the war for a few hours. Drink was one option and in December 1940 the city's Chief Constable noted disapprovingly that members of the armed forces, particularly the RAF, were 'having more than is good for them. There has been a large increase in the number of women frequenting public houses.'[98] Entertainment was also available at the city's theatres, dance halls or cinemas although Oxford apparently had a bad name among servicemen because its cinema prices were so high.[99]

In Bicester the YMCA provided a marquee in Rookery Field for Forces' recreation in 1941 and this was eventually replaced by a temporary hut. After local effort had raised £5,000, a new building of concrete blocks was built in Bennett's Close off Chapel Street, and opened in September 1943, providing a canteen, rest and recreation rooms and a library.[100] From November 1939 a Benson Services Canteen was open seven days a week throughout the war and was staffed by at least eighty-six volunteer helpers, all but two of them female. In January 1945 each committee member was given an illuminated address by the airmen, airwomen and corporals of the Photographic Section, Royal Air Force, Benson, as 'a token of appreciation of the hospitality extended by your Committee at the CANTEEN, and the many kindnesses shewn by all the helpers there'.[101]

The *Oxford Mail* published a letter from 'Four Desert Rats' in September 1944 alleging that 'the people of Oxford have had a very comfortable war' and complaining that one ungrateful woman had remarked that 'she wished it was peace-time so they could be rid of us'.[102] The city and the county had, in a sense, been distant spectators of a struggle that was going on elsewhere, but there were few communities or households without a more intense and personal interest in the outcome. From Woodcote seventy-three men had gone to fight for their country, and out of a population of 543 at Binfield Heath, Thomas Scotcher estimated that no fewer than 121 men and women were in the armed forces at Christmas 1944. At the Henbest home George and Frank were in the Army, Ted in the Navy and Bob in the RAF; of the two sons-in-law, one was in the RAF and the other was a Government horticulturist. The father, a veteran of the First World War, was a member of the Home Guard.[103]

The airgraph letter, transmitted on microfilm from the furthest corners of the world and then printed out for delivery through the post, maintained contact between servicemen and women and the people they had left behind. This is one such letter sent by Private Cyril Garlick to Mrs Olive Thompson of Radcliffe Road, Oxford, in September 1942:

My Dear Olive & all

Thank you so much for yours of Aug 31st received yesterday, good going on your part too Olive, I have just sent Bertha a pair of stockings so when I have finished night duty & I can get into town I will get you a pair. I will look forward to having the tennis balls.

It would be grand if I could get home for Xmas, but as you say one never can tell what will happen next.

Very strange that Bill should have that queer feeling about the same time, but I am glad it passed off. . . .

I have got the snaps I had taken so I will send you one, I cannot get any films for my camera at the moment, and the fellow said he was lucky to get one for his.

And so for the present I leave you,
Yours very sincerely
Cyril XXXXX[104]

In many households there inevitably existed a daily fear of the official letter like this one, received by J.R. Bunning of Earl Street, Oxford, in August 1940:

Dear Sir,

I regret to inform you that your son No. 753067 Leading Aircraftman Ernest Jack BUNNING, Royal Air Force, was seriously wounded during an enemy air raid on the 16th August 1940 and he has been admitted to the Radcliffe Infirmary, Oxford.
   Any change in his condition will be notified to me, and you will be informed immediately.[105]

Other households experienced the mixed emotions of receiving letters from sons or husbands who were now prisoners of war. Mr and Mrs J. Bannister of King's End, Bicester, were so pleased to get a letter from their son in a Japanese prisoner of war camp in Taiwan that they had it published in the *Bicester Advertiser* in July 1943:

Dear mother and dad, hoping you are well and the others, as I am in the best of health. The food is good and we are treated very well. We get a small wage and cigs, and the billets are good. From your loving son, Arthur.[106]
   At No. 119 Kynaston Road, Didcot, joy must have been mixed with tears in December 1943 when Mrs Lou Crisford and her five-year-old son, John, received a Christmas letter from her husband in Stalag 383:

Prisoners of war from the 9th Battalion, Oxfordshire and Buckinghamshire Light Infantry in Stalag XXa, 1940.

My Dearest Lou and John, Here's answer to yours dear of 16/10 received 3/12 the first one from you for a month but I have heard from nobody else and no parcels of any kind, they must be held up somewhere. I hope you and John are O.K. and have a very happy birthday also to Dad I am writing a card to Mum. The weather here is a devil and the camp has been a sea of mud but it is not so bad now as it has frozen up. By the way dear you sent in the last parcel a tin of pears brilliantine I find it comes in very useful for rubbing on my hands and face for chapps. . . . Yes Darling I should love to be with John and talk with him he must be very quaint. . . . I do hope my darling you enjoy yourself And I hope next Christmas we shall be together again. Well I will dry up now remember I love you Darling and give our son a big one.

Criss XX[107]

The policy of encouraging communities to adopt a warship added a broader dimension to these personal hopes and fears. Oxford, for example, adopted HMS

Engineers building a pontoon bridge across the River Thames at Shillingford during the Spartan Exercise in March 1943.

Enterprise in 1943 and the local press was able to announce proudly that the vessel was involved in shelling the shore batteries of Cherbourg in June 1944.[108] Witney Rural District's destroyer, HMS *Aldenham*, was sunk in January 1945 and Banbury's HMS *Harvester* was torpedoed by a U-boat in May 1943, but even these disasters brought the realities of war into sharper focus and instances of individual heroism provided a source of 'local' pride. In November 1943 Banbury decided to adopt the Free French ship *Aconit*, which had gone to *Harvester*'s assistance when it was sunk.[109]

Although Oxfordshire seemed so remote from the battle line, it was claimed in September 1944 that the bombardment of ports in the Boulogne area could be faintly heard in Oxford.[110] The county was spared the ravages of war, but had been much changed physically first by the spread of anti-invasion defences and then by the construction of new airfields and army camps, and improvements to local railways. The defensive preparations were never tested, but the county had an important role as part of the springboard from which the Second Front was launched against Hitler in June 1944. The people of Oxfordshire who were not themselves in the armed forces witnessed and became involved in this military build-up, retaining for the rest of their lives vivid memories both good and bad. For children, the sheer excitement of it all emerges from the pages of the Albury and Tiddington School log-book during Exercise Spartan in 1943:

> Mar. 10. . . . At recess and noon the children went to watch Can[adian] soldiers who gave them biscuits, stamps, tins of beef, etc. . . .

> Mar. 11. Children still excited by Army manoeuvres in the district.[111]

CHAPTER FIVE

Home Guard

As the German Blitzkrieg swept into France in May 1940 and forced the British Expeditionary Force back towards the English Channel, the country faced an imminent invasion. On 14 May Anthony Eden, the Secretary of State for War, broadcast an appeal for the immediate formation of a force to be known as 'Local Defence Volunteers', and requested males aged between seventeen and sixty-five to report for enrolment at their local police station.[1]

There were fears that the response might be limited because of the number of volunteers already involved in ARP work, but any such doubts were allayed within days of the appeal. In Oxford hundreds of men answered the call and at times there were queues outside the police station in Banbury.[2] By 17 May the *Bicester Advertiser* was reporting large numbers of volunteers to counter 'The menace of the parachute jumper'; already there had been 98 enrolments in Bicester, 47 in Kidlington, 18 in Islip and 2 in Finmere.[3] At Fyfield regulars in the White Hart had previously discussed the problem of dealing with enemy paratroops and one had suggested, 'hand it over to members of the British Legion. All these ex-servicemen, armed, would deal with any paratroops.' Eden's appeal a few days later virtually echoed his words and the establishment of a Fyfield and Tubney Platoon of the LDV was assured. Since the village had no police station 'a night was fixed for the Sergeant of Police from Cumnor to come and enrol members. A good number were enrolled and some time later formally sworn-in at Tubney School by Captain Cheshire, who was in charge of the Frilford area.'[4]

The volunteers were from a wide spectrum of society and some were so keen to join that they took little notice of the upper age limit. The Oxford contingent was of course unusual in including so many professors and senior members of the University who were soon to be found in almost every rank. Dr G.S. Gordon, a former Vice-Chancellor and President of Magdalen College, became a private and Dr C.M. Bowra, Warden of Wadham, a lieutenant; other lieutenants included Dr T. Parker, Keeper of the Ashmolean Museum, and Dr Douglas Veale, the University Registrar. Lord Elton became a sergeant and the Head of the Geological Department, J.A. Douglas, became Colonel and Commanding Officer of the battalion.[5] Around Thame members of the South Oxfordshire Hunt found a new use for their horsemanship and, along the Thames, knowledgeable fishermen and boating enthusiasts were invited to join the Upper Thames Patrol, covering the river between Lechlade and Teddington.[6] In Burford LDV volunteers included many farmworkers, lorry drivers and even an MP; at Fyfield and Tubney the platoon claimed to be typical of any in the country:

Behind the Regular Army; the stalwarts of Sibford Home Guard during the war.

Who were we? Well, our platoon was representative of any platoon in the country. There was Tom, Tommy, Teddie, Charlie, Jackie, and Les. Percy, Bill, Harry, Thomas, Tommy, Jim, and Donald. 'Tiger', Frank, 'Bungo'. Dickie, John, 'Trooper' and 'Old Dick'. Bern, Ernie, Owen, Mike, 'Old Bill', and Arthur. Good old English names. Their jobs? Carpenters, masons, labourers, carters, shepherds, gardeners, bakers, game-keepers, woodmen, farmworkers, storemen, farmers, quarrymen, grocers. A good country collection.[7]

The role of the new force was at first unclear and it was exposed to early ridicule by a chronic lack of uniform and equipment. The volunteers were at first nicknamed 'Parashots' because their role was thought to be restricted to watching out for, reporting on and rounding up enemy parachutists. Other nicknames followed the issue of the first 'uniforms', armlets bearing the letters LDV, which were issued to just ten out of fifty or sixty men in the Abingdon contingent on 25 May. Men speculated as to whether the letters stood for 'Long Dentured Veterans' or 'Last Desperate Venture'; unkinder souls decided that they meant 'Look, Duck and Vanish'.[8] In June the Mayor of Oxford, Ald. C.J.V. Bellamy, described the local force as being responsible not only for dealing with paratroops but also for defending the city.[9] Elsewhere, the LDV tried enthusiastically to prepare for probable invasion. Gun slits were fashioned in a Cotswold stone garden wall at Shipton-under-Wychwood to control the approaches to Fiveways. At Woodcote volunteers under Major Brownlow built road-blocks at strategic points; County Council roadmen at Kingham dug trenches across the verges on the approach roads and helped to construct sandbagged firing points while the LDV built 'knife-rests', cross-legged barriers covered with barbed wire. Their first defensive position at Trigmoor Turn was, however, roundly dismissed by a visiting 'brass hat' as being 'of no use whatever, except as a decoy'.[10] Abingdon too began to receive direction from above:

> We learnt that each village was called a 'nodal point', why was a mystery until it was explained that the whole country was covered by the LDV as with a net, and the villages . . . were the knots. At these points we were to fight, and so deny the use of the roads to the enemy. In order to do this we constructed road-blocks and, ostrich like, felt reasonably secure behind them, although they were of the flimsiest nature and would not have caused any inconvenience to a Jeep, had there been any about in those days. Brasshats appeared, disapproved of the siting of most of them and ordered last night's sweated labour to be done all over again TO-NIGHT – 'tomorrow may be TOO LATE'. A day or two later a 'high up' with other ideas disapproved of the new siting.[11]

The volunteers at Kingham enjoyed monitoring traffic and pedestrians at their new road-block, but one man lost some credibility when his gruff challenge received the breezy reply, 'It's only me, darling' from his wife. In Headington a member of one patrol caused some surprise by asking to see a passer-by's identity card and giving the man his gun while he checked the document. On another occasion there was embarrassment for both parties when a sentry stopped a young woman cyclist at a road-block and forgot what he was supposed to ask for; his colleagues were doubtless convulsed with laughter as he said, 'Sorry, miss, but I want to see your – your – your – er, what's-name, please'.[12]

During the summer of 1940 the duties and organization of the LDV were gradually formalized. In July the force was renamed the Home Guard at Winston Churchill's suggestion and it was restructured along the lines of the Regular Army on 3 August; the Home Guard was subsequently organized by county, battalion, company and platoon so that the Abingdon platoon, for example, became No. 3 Platoon, A Company, 1st Berkshire (Abingdon) Battalion.[13] The new structure integrated separate factory and workplace units such as the one that had been recruited at John Allen & Sons in Cowley by Major Allen.[14] The main functions of the Home Guard were defined as observation and information, but in case of invasion, it would also have provided an initial military response. Later Operational Instructions contained the chilling warning:

> Static troops in the Oxfordshire Sub-District will hold their allotted positions to the last man and the last round, to enable the Field Army to destroy the enemy. Mobile units in Oxfordshire Sub-District will, within their prescribed areas of activity, harass and delay the enemy with the same purpose.[15]

Members of the Home Guard everywhere became accustomed to patrolling vulnerable sites such as water towers, gasworks, road and railway bridges and level crossings. In Bicester this probably seemed less dangerous than patrolling the grounds of the Garth where Mrs Keith-Falconer kept a number of huge deerhounds and great danes; one cautious soldier refused to take the early duty,

Members of the Home Guard platoon formed by John Allen & Son improve their shooting in the gravel pit at Burcot near Dorchester.

saying, 'I am not going out there until those bloody great hounds have had their breakfast'.[16] At Benson the Home Guard kept the telephone exchange under observation and, if there was an enemy attack, they were to act as guides for regular troops and to destroy petrol pumps at civilian garages. The local unit of the Upper Thames Patrol carried out motorboat patrols between Benson and Clifton Hampden from its headquarters at the Shillingford Bridge Hotel; these patrols kept in regular touch with units at Abingdon and Wallingford and their duties included examining boats, inspecting identity cards, checking for wireless sets and reporting enemy landings on the river.[17] At Westwell Sir Sothern Holland 'used to patrol the lanes at night on horseback, especially the western cross-roads, with Fairfax-Lucy or his groom Jack Baguley, now over 70 years old'.[18] Mounted patrols were also active around Thame where the South Oxfordshire Hunt Troop was committed to the following duties during an enemy offensive:

Burford High Street in 1943, showing the wheel and tree barriers which the Home Guard used as road blocks.

To occupy points of vantage outside the town or village defences, so as to deny such points to the enemy, and to harass them by sniping.

To watch country outside the village defences, and between observation posts, or specially dangerous areas, such as woodlands and dead ground which cannot be observed by stationary patrols.

The patrols would also assist in keeping open communications outside the village defences, should telephone wires be cut.[19]

On many of these patrols there were few excitements, but Robert Willis was moved to write a poem, 'The Bells', by one incident in Eynsham:

> 'Twas on a silent starry night
> When the nation was at war,
> Old Tom Gritt and I was in the Guards,
> And we was on patrol.
>
> Way up the Witney Road we was,
> Beyond the 'Evenlode'
> Invasion in the minds of all
> It were a heavy load.
>
> Then all at once we heard the bells
> From over 'Sow-Leigh' way,
> And both our hearts just missed a beat,
> And a deadly fear held sway.

I looks at Tom – Tom looks at I,
Then cast our gaze into the sky;
Tom seized the bolt of his trusty gun
And rammed the shell full home.
Then I of course just followed suit
We knew the time had come!

'Thee's got one up thur has thee lad?
'Hast got one up the spout?'
And then he whips his bayonet out,
Nigh half as long as Tom . . .

'Twas then we heard that dreaded roar
From the silent starlit night,
We knew the Hun was watching us
And gathering all his might.

He saw the glint of our bayonet,
For Tom and I was marching yet;
His heart must then have turned to stone
As he turned his plane – to head for home.

'Fuhrer, Fuhrer, do not come,
They are ready here, and will not run';
So ran the message from the sky,
As he sees old Tom – and then sees I!

They told us it were a false alarm,
'Return to your factory, field or farm';
But Tom and I both knew full well
That night we heard the Sow-Leigh bell,
'Twas us as turned the Nazi might
On that dark and silent, starlit night![20]

The Home Guard was viewed with a good deal of amusement, by the volunteers themselves as well as by outsiders, because it was so badly equipped in these early months. Bicester was fortunate in that its company included some members of the local rifle club, but the general shortage of weapons led to the proposal to issue units with pikes consisting of about 4 to 5 ft of metal pipe with a bayonet welded on to the end.[21] The Home Guard in the Bartons was at first armed with an assortment of sticks, .22 rifles, shotguns, pikes and rubber truncheons; the platoon which covered Cassington, Begbroke and Yarnton

had one rifle and ten rounds of ammo – between the three villages – when we started, which was very awkward, because this rifle etc. had to be handed over to the next patrol. . . .[22]

At Kingham, home-made Molotov cocktails were made by filling whisky or port bottles with inflammable liquid and another ingenious attempt to remedy the lack of weaponry is perhaps recalled by a notice in the *Thame Gazette* in July 1940:

B Company of the 1st Berkshire Battalion Home Guard marching along Ock Street in Abingdon.

WANTED Hundreds of discarded GIRLS' STOCKINGS, for use in local defence. Please hand to any member of the LDV.

The Home Guard was scarcely ready for invasion, but in Kingham at least arrangements had been made to ring the church bells if enemy parachutists were seen:

> For this purpose the key of the church tower door was kept under the leaning tombstone of Thomas Buzzard 1849. This was supposed to be known only to the Rector and to the Home Guard.[23]

Weapons were gradually provided and the Abingdon platoon, for example, recalled 31 May 1940 as a red-letter day:

> We received our first issue of rifles. The scale it is true was only about four per hundred men and ten rounds per rifle. Rifles which had been immersed in grease for a quarter of a century, and a very considerable amount of which was transferred to our clothes every time we handled them, in spite of the hours spent in vain efforts to remove it. However the process of being armed had started, as had the howl for more, . . . so much so that anyone from 'higher up' who came to visit us . . . always began when yet afar off, 'No, I hav'nt brought you any rifles, but . . .'.[24]

After a few months American .300 calibre rifles, Remingtons, Eddystones and Winchesters, were issued, although at Burford the pleasure of receipt was again tarnished by the 'dreadful task' of removing the thick layer of yellow grease in

Home Guard parade in the Market Square at Chipping Norton in May 1943.

which they had been stored.[25] The potential fire-power of the Barton Home Guard was further increased in September 1940 when it received a Lewis gun and two Browning Automatic Rifles.[26]

Denim uniforms began to replace the LDV armlets, the first batch reaching Abingdon on 15 June:

> The triumph was however shortlived, it soon being discovered that 'suits' of Denim was a misnomer, there being no relationship between a blouse and a pair of trousers marked with the same size numbers. It was also apparent that we must all be either giants or midgets, which is perhaps why it was left to us to fix the buttons and clips, so laboriously counted out and signed for at HQ, but never all present and correct when we came to do our tailoring. Each blouse . . . and each pair of trousers had to be tried on, it was no use going by the size numbers or the dimensions on the label. In some instances it would have been more appropriate to put the size of the collar on the trousers. Out of the eleven suits, perhaps three men could be more or less reasonably attired, the remainder either having their nether garments folded round them or appearing with extremely decollete blouses.[27]

This experience was repeated in the Bartons in August when 'The reception of this uniform, the language which greeted it and the sight of the wearers will never be realized by anyone not in the HG in 1940'.[28] Serge uniforms were at last issued early in 1941, giving the organization a much more military appearance.[29] By May 1941 the Officer Commanding Oxford City Home Guard was receiving this almost unqualified praise from the Zone Commander, Colonel E.T. Chamberlayne:

I wish to congratulate you and all members of your Battalion on yesterday's parade. The arms were handled well, the men stood steady on parade and the turn out was good. It was obvious that a great deal of effort had been made by all concerned.

The above made all the more patent the failure of the O.C. South Ward Coy. to turn out properly dressed. If he found a difficulty in so doing there was nothing to prevent his handing over to his second in command and absenting himself from the parade.

I suggest that if you think well, this Officer should be given leave of absence until such time as he gives up command of his Company.

The officer concerned is thought to have been Frank Pakenham, later Lord Longford, who was in the process of relinquishing command to Maurice Bowra, the Warden of Wadham College[30].

From the first it was essential that the Home Guard should be trained up as an effective fighting force. Training films, demonstrations and a flood of official books and pamphlets provided background instruction in many topics. On a practical level, arms drill was often the province of ex-infantrymen in a platoon and those with an aptitude for training might be sent to Cowley Barracks in order to extend their knowledge and pass it on. Shooting practice for Oxford Companies was held at the Barracks or Slade Camp while live bomb-throwing took place on a battalion range in Old Road, fashioned out of a former brick field; a disused gravel pit at Burcot was another location for bomb-throwing. The 'Highlands' Platoon, covering the high ground around Southfield golf-course, created its own miniature rifle range to improve the men's efficiency and stage competitive events.[31] At Kingham the Home Guard held shooting practices at

A Browning machine-gun team looks less than confident during a Home Guard training camp in Sutton Courtenay in September 1941. In the background, their sergeant talks to King George VI who was paying a brief visit to the camp.

Mr Eaton's orchard gravel pit, being trained by NCOs from the 5th King's Regiment while it was based at Adlestrop Park after Dunkirk.[32] A mortar-firing practice at Bicester nearly had disastrous consequences:

All went well until we had a stoppage with one of these mortars and, as the bomb did not fire, we retired a safe distance of thirty yards or so and waited for the grenade to explode. After three or four minutes deadly silence the voice of Major Fane bellowed out 'What the hell are you all waiting for?' When I explained that there was a stoppage in the barrel he marched up to the offending mortar, put his arm down the barrel and pulled out the bomb and hurled it some thirty yards when it immediately exploded, on impact. I knew then why he was known as the 'mad major'![33]

More extensive training exercises aimed to develop the military skills that the Home Guard would require if the threatened invasion took place. These could serve to demonstrate the crucial importance of local knowledge as, for example, when 'enemy paratroopers' represented by men from Taynton were being hunted by Burford Home Guard:

In the course of their search one squad were going along the river bank when an old private said suddenly: 'Look up on top of that pollard willow.' Result – the two most important 'enemies' were pulled down and made prisoners. When asked, later, what made him suspect the willow tree, the old inhabitant replied: 'I used to hide in that there tree when I was a boy!'[34]

Things did not always go according to plan, however, and a Ledwell Home Guard recalled an occasion when a group of men were looking for the enemy:

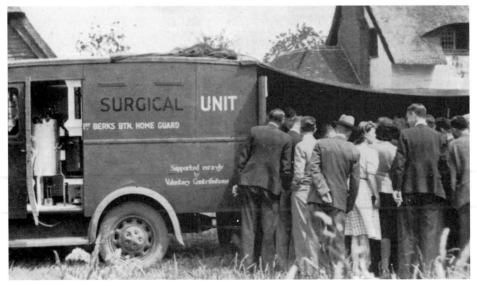

An interested crowd gathers round the Mobile Surgical Unit, a field hospital for Home Guards or the civilian population which was unique to the 1st Berkshire Battalion Home Guard.

'What's that over by that hedge!'
   (Man with binoculars): 'Just a sheep.'
   It was the Platoon Commander crawling up the ditch on all fours. (The said PC being over seventy years old and considered too old for the job.)[35]

During an exercise when Fyfield and Tubney platoon was attacking Kingston Bagpuize a squad commander fell into a hole and gypsies' dogs gave away the position of one patrol; there was more humour when a cow's swishing tail was mistaken for the dot-dash movement of a flag when a platoon was practising signal flashes. In a large-scale exercise at Faringdon, trouble ensued as

One ruffled, harassed, but very determined, defender was insisting that he had 'shot' one of the attackers whilst crossing the road; this was being hotly denied, and the argument grew so heated that both contestants 'downed rifles' and sought decision by fisticuffs, the fight starting at a front garden gate of a cottage, proceeded up the short path and finally right into the 'front parlour' of an amazed housewife who had been standing at her open door watching the men 'playing at soldiers'.[36]

For the 'Highlands' Platoon from Oxford an operational march to Horton-cum-Studley provided a memorable day:

The venue was reached soon after 'opening time', where much liquid refreshment was partaken and enjoyed. Thanks to 'mine host' (Mr Grant) a very excellent outdoor lunch was provided, and when the effects had worn off an exercise was staged with the necessary effects. Returning to the 'King's Arms' for a light tea, the return journey was successfully completed, with the exception of a few minor casualties, in excellent fettle.[37]

For some years the Home Guard tended to be dismissed as a possible substitute for regular troops. Thus, on 5 February 1942, Company Commanders from the Oxford City Battalion attended a meeting at which

OC (Officer Commanding) troops Oxford gave details of new Operation Orders. The regular troops which it was proposed to put in the front lines, manning Road Blocks on Witney, Woodstock and Banbury Roads proved to be C3 batmen and cooks devoid of modern weapons and physically incapable, according to their officers of marching 3 miles. It was pointed out that this was hardly a compliment to the Home Guard.[38]

From the summer of 1941, however, Kingham Home Guard held many exercises with army units and the efficiency of the force was improved by training camps such as the one which the Abingdon company held at Sutton Courtenay over the August Bank Holiday weekend in the same year; this was said to have been the first such camp held by the Home Guard and it was visited on the Sunday by King George VI.[39] In Oxford an assault course was opened in Jackdaw Lane in 1942 and 'negotiating the well-thought out scheme of obstacles' was recalled as both useful and pleasurable by Sgt. Bint of the 'Highlands' Platoon.

The Mayor of Oxford inspects Home Guards in Broad Street prior to a service at the city church of St Martin and All Saints on Whit Sunday 1941.

The new facility also improved another aspect of training:

> Realism in exercises was added to some extent by the issue of 'Cracker-blank' in imitation of rifle fire, and 'Thunderflashes' to represent larger detonations. Hitherto the absence of 'effects' had somewhat dulled the proper staging of sham fights, except for the ingenuity of members in preparing home-made bombs. . . .[40]

Local Home Guard units took part in the Battle of Oxford exercise at the end of January 1943, helping to check the advance of American 'enemy' troops at Boars Hill very effectively. A feint by a small patrol lured the American infantry away from their armoured cars and tanks and into a wood where they were

> in full view of something like eighty defenders, all camouflaged and hidden. They came forward as a couple of outposts withdrew and threw thunderflashes and claybombs into the undergrowth. Had they been the real things the

grenadiers would have suffered far heavier casualties than those being attacked. Then, suddenly, all hell broke loose. Mines went up, hundreds of blanks were fired, thunderflashes were thrown, and the advancing infantry came full tilt into it, and into the man-traps that had been so carefully prepared for them. The umpires gave us fifty per cent of the attack casualties at once. The tanks, hearing the din, nosed round the corner, and were confronted by a huge mound of straw across the road, which burst into flames as they moved forward. This halted them all right, and in the ensuing mix-up, Lt. Hill crept up under cover and shot the crew of one of the armoured cars before they knew he was in the vicinity.[41]

As the risk of invasion diminished and the Army prepared to open the second front against Germany, the Home Guard gradually took over a range of military duties. In March 1943 volunteers were therefore being sought for the Oxford Home Guard Anti-Aircraft Battery which was going to involve each man doing one night's duty per week.[42] A year later the Military Police were withdrawn from Leafield Wireless Station and Home Guards from Leafield and Kingham subsequently helped to defend it.[43]

Much of the Home Guard's work was inevitably mundane and unalluring, and E.J. Lainchbury recorded that, after the first flush of enthusiasm, the Kingham force could be divided into two camps, the 'keen' and the 'not keen'.[44] In April

Over the wire; Oxford Home Guards negotiate one of the obstacles on the Jackdaw Lane assault course which opened in 1942.

1941 there were unfilled vacancies in the Banbury Home Guard following the call-up of some of its men and four women were needed

> to give part-time services in connection with a carrier pigeon service, now being organized. Their duties would be to assist with the birds and be available in case of emergency.[45]

Initially, women's interest in the Home Guard had been discouraged, and a telegram sent by the South Midland Area Headquarters to Oxford City LDV on 11 June 1940 warned:

> Women cannot be enrolled in the LDV. Any driving by women will be voluntary and at their own risk.

As in other areas, however, the shortage of men encouraged a change of heart and a unit of the Women's Home Defence Corps, popularly known as the Women's Home Guard, was established in Oxford in June 1942. The founder of the Corps, Dr Edith Summerskill, told the audience that it was not 'an army of Amazons armed with rifles' and that it was principally to be used to replace men in the roles of signalling, camouflage, barricading, first aid, intelligence work and field cooking. Nevertheless, members also learned self-defence and unarmed combat, and in July 1942 women from the Headington Corps received instruction about rifles and Mills bombs.[46]

The introduction of women in a support role was not enough, however, and the Government found it necessary to introduce compulsory service for males in November 1941 . To some extent, this simply reinforced the 'not keen' element who were not necessarily impressed by the prospect of winning attendance cups and proficiency badges or participating in football or miniature rifle competitions.[47] An eighteen-year-old lorry driver was fined in Oxford in August 1943 after explaining to the court that 'I have no time to join the Home Guard'. In February an Appleton Home Guard was brought to book for failing to attend parades; the court was told that he had

> joined the Home Guard on 27 May 1942 and parades of his platoon were held every Thursday evening and Sunday morning. Owing to the irregularity of his attendances the company commander visited him on 22 November and handed him a notice ordering him to attend. This did not have the desired effect and at subsequent parades he was asked why he had been absent. His excuses were not reasonable . . . [he] was absent from parade on 26 November, his excuse being that his intention was to attend every other parade. As he was absent on 10 December he was asked on the following parade for a reason and he said he had been to the films at Abingdon. He then missed three parades, his excuse being that it was raining.[48]

If slackness like this was probably uncommon there was clearly less incentive to attend parades as the tide of war turned in the Allies' favour, and the small number participating in the 'Highlands' Platoon 1944 Camp at Wytham was 'definitely disappointing' to the organizers.[49] Guards were withdrawn from key

Crowds watch and buses wait as the Oxford Home Guard marches through The Plain. On this occasion at least, officers and men seem to have been out of step with each other.

sites in Oxford such as Pressed Steel and the gas and electricity works during August 1944; on 10 September the 'wheel and tree' road-blocks were last used in Kingham and County Council workmen took them away in the following month.[50] The Home Guard had served its purpose and the call to 'Stand-down' was received on 1 November, leading to final battalion parades in early December. The Bartons platoon was left with no fewer than fourteen files of printed, cyclostyled or typed papers:

> there were reams of instructions, orders, forms, returns, subsistence claims, travelling claims, ammunition returns, etc., not forgetting cancellations and amendments.

At the platoon's 'Stand-down' dinner at the Star in Bicester on 3 January 1945, Private Price preferred to recall the spirit in which the Home Guard had been formed:

In 1940 when the whole world shook,
Hitler turned to Britain with a very nasty look,
So Eden asked for Volunteers to join the LDV.
The butcher, baker, barrister, chimney sweep and me.
Up and down the country they rallied to the flag
You can bet your bottom button that Barton didn't lag.

We said we'd roam the roads at night instead of going to bed,
We were a desperate little party with Major Fleming at our head.
We walked about with twelve bore guns and little four point tens,
We hadn't any rifles and we hadn't any Stens.
I don't know how we managed to guard the fields and farms
With little else but LDV badges on our arms.
But still we said we'd do our best to guard it yard by yard,
They dropped the title LDV and called us the Home Guard.

They made us look like soldiers in brand new khaki suits,
Haversacks and water-bottles and a pair of heavy boots.
Then they gave us rifles with bayonets on the ends,
Lewis Guns and Brownings and a useful lot of Stens.
Our officers and NCO's would learn us how to shoot
We would stop old Jerry coming to England for his loot.[51]

CHAPTER SIX

War Work

While the armed forces were engaged in direct combat with the enemy, virtually all of the civilian population was enlisted in a vital support role, providing the necessary munitions, food and supplies that would help to win the war. As in the First World War, the absence of so many men on military service led to the large-scale employment of women in new areas of work, and volunteers young and old also played an important part in the war effort. In Oxfordshire, as elsewhere, the slogan was 'It All Depends On Me'.

The outbreak of war brought initial disruption to many businesses as men joined the services and peacetime markets disappeared. The building trade was badly hit and engineers, garage owners, furniture makers, warehousemen and dealers suddenly found themselves with spare capacity. At Cowley car production ceased immediately and more than half the workforce of 5,000 left Morris Motors either to join up or to look for other work.[1] Unemployment became a serious issue and a group of dignitaries headed by Lord Bicester, the Lord Lieutenant of Oxfordshire, campaigned for a programme of public works and urged the Government to take the local employment position into account when placing contracts.[2]

The problem was gradually resolved by the change-over to war production. The Air Ministry had designated Cowley as one of six depots for the repair of aircraft in March 1939, the others to be run directly by the RAF. Soon after war broke out, Lord Nuffield and his colleagues were able to argue successfully that private industry could undertake all this work and that repairs could be divided into classes and allocated to specialist firms within the area of each depot. Nuffield was asked to implement his own advice and was given the title Director-General of Maintenance, RAF. Cowley became the headquarters of the whole Civilian Repair Organization (CRO) and also its No. 1 Civilian Repair Unit (CRU). The CRO had the urgent task of establishing four other repair depots to serve the rest of the country and it gradually built up an extensive network of smaller repair units. Firms with civil aviation experience formed major suppliers to the CRUs, but the motor trade also proved invaluable because of its empty stockrooms and under-employed repair shops.[3] In Oxford, for example, the spacious Botley Road premises of City Motors

immediately attracted the Ministry of Aircraft Production, a large portion being devoted to the repair of fighter aircraft under a Civilian Repair Organization contract. . . . A special machine shop was installed to take care of Ministry . . . machining contracts and many thousands of aircraft parts were produced.[4]

Lord Nuffield talks to the test pilot of a rebuilt Hurricane outside the Flight Sheds at Cowley Airfield on 4 June 1940. During the crucial months of the Battle of Britain, Cowley returned 150 seriously damaged planes to action.

Airfields had to be established beside the major depots, and on 1 October 1939 H.W.B. Joseph expressed the City Council's considerable irritation with the choice of site in Cowley:

> Yesterday morning . . . I learnt that the Air Ministry was commandeering half the site we have acquired for a new Junior & Infant School in Church Cowley. There is none of our proposed new schools more urgently required. The site was acquired only after great difficulty, & there is no other suitable; yet this is done without any enquiry or consultation. It is supposed that the motor works are to make instruments of war – presumably aeroplanes – there is open ground westward between the site & the works; whether that is to be built on or to be a landing ground I have no idea. But is it wise to make of Oxford, with its historic buildings, a legitimate target for bombers?[5]

The city's protests went unheeded and the construction of Cowley airfield was completed in the spring of 1940. No. 1 CRU received its first consignment of damaged planes in November 1939 and repairs to the initial batch of Spitfires and Hurricanes took six months before successful test flights were held at RAF Abingdon. The fall of France in May 1940 and the threat of air raids on Cowley encouraged the CRO to move its headquarters staff of about 200 people to Merton College. The number of employees at the CRU rose swiftly from 800 in May to 1,200 in August, including many workers who had come to Oxford for safety. At the same time, the output of planes repaired each week by the CRO across the country soared from 20 before Dunkirk to 97 in early June and 160 by mid-July. Fighter pilots sometimes flew their damaged machines straight to Cowley airfield:

At teatime – 4.15 p.m., July 20th, 1940 – a Spitfire, which was obviously in distress, landed on the airfield without any previous warning. 'Take my machine to the out-patients' department and have her put right,' the pilot said. 'I'll wait.'

Official working hours were from 8 a.m. to 10 p.m. but, in crisis conditions, work often went on round the clock with exhausted employees snatching a few hours' sleep in a corner of the workshop:

Men living in distant villages would arrive by the milk lorries, three hours before they were due, because there were no 'buses to bring them to Cowley, and if they were late their particular 'gang' of fifteen to twenty workers would be immobilised.

The workers looked pale and felt their weariness most in the early morning, but as each day wore on they forgot everything except the need for speed. Britain's battle was waiting for them. Whenever a 'plane had to be turned around or over, a shout would come for assistance and twenty pairs of hands were soon helping.

Helped by this teamwork, No. 1 CRU was able to return 150 seriously damaged aircraft to active service during the crucial months of the Battle of Britain. The repaired planes were tested over Cowley and one of the test pilots' favourite tricks was to dive between the chimneys of Morris Motors and Pressed Steel at about 400 m.p.h. Local people sometimes complained about planes skimming their rooftops and a notice on the airfield warned: 'To all pilots. No low flying or diving or "shooting up" the girl friend over Oxford. Be warned!'[6]

A tremendous team spirit was also evident at Witney aerodrome where De Havilland had relocated its service and repair facilities in late 1939 after being forced to leave Hatfield. Operating as a CRU, De Havilland employed over 1,200 people to repair and renovate its own aircraft, and from 1941–2 Hurricanes and Spitfires as well. In the winter of 1940 employees donned overcoats and gloves to undertake urgent work in two storage hangars that had no heating and inadequate light. John Dossett-Davies recalled:

There was a sense of belonging, a common identity – it was a true community even though the hours for the juvenile workers were 8 a.m. to 5.30 p.m. five days a week with compulsory overtime three Saturdays out of four, and two evenings a week. Adult workers sometimes did two shifts straight off. In the early days for some months people worked at the crisis level – 7 days a week and every night overtime. Later it was an alternative 6 and 5 day week with lots of compulsory overtime. . . . Perhaps one of the best examples of the De Havilland 'spirit' was Easter 1943. A Squadron of Spitfires was flown in late on the Thursday afternoon. They were dismantled, serviced, overhauled, crated, packed and despatched to the USSR all over the Easter weekend. Some men worked the day shift then round the clock on the following night shift then went home for 2–3 hours then returned and worked the second day shift without any real sleep. So fast was this accomplished that the workers went forward to meet the planes as they taxied in, so keen were they to do this work. In fact, the Squadron Leader's plane which he was due to fly back to his Squadron later in the day was partially dismantled in error while he was at tea!

By the end of the war, De Havilland CRU had repaired and returned to service over 700 Spitfires and Hurricanes and more than 800 of the company's own aircraft.[7] From its Oxford headquarters, the CRO managed the repair of 80,000 aircraft throughout the country, entirely confirming the wisdom of Lord Nuffield's advice in 1939.[8]

As well as being the home of No. 1 CRU, Cowley accommodated No. 50 Maintenance Unit (MU) and one of the country's two Metal and Produce

A transporter arrives at Cowley with the remains of the Messerschmitt Me110 flown to Britain in 1941 by Rudolf Hess, Hitler's Deputy. A few Oxford people saw the 'Top Secret' plane displayed briefly in St Giles' before it was whisked away.

Recovery Depots (MPRDs). No. 50 MU was a salvage organization which sent out gangs of men to collect and deliver crashed aircraft to repair workshops and depots, and to take wreckage to other factories for 'cannibalization'. Ernest Fairfax described it as 'the first, the largest and, in the latter stages of the war, the only surviving civilian manned unit in the RAF'.[9] The men were on call seven days a week and were often away from home for long periods. Food was not easy to come by and Denis Gibson remembered having to kill a rabbit with a stick near Okehampton when returning from Cornwall with a crashed German bomber; next day, a woman at a nearby lodge made a rabbit pie which, with swede and potatoes, had to suffice for a gang of about ten men. The job could also be extremely dangerous and Arthur Conners, the carpenter of a gang at White Waltham airfield, had a narrow escape when a sudden raid resulted in a piece of shrapnel passing clean through his saw.[10] More persistent danger was faced by a gang trying to clear crashed planes from an aerodrome in south-east England on 25 September 1940:

> The 'drome was a mass of craters, some measuring 50 ft by 100 ft across, and thousands of incendiaries covered the ground like mushrooms. On one occasion I counted 5 aircraft burning on the ground close to us and one Junkers 88, with two Spitfires on his tail, was driven down just over our heads, when it burst into flames and crashed close by, killing all the occupants.
>
> All through the hours of daylight Jerry was very busy and things were getting exciting, as 'planes were falling all around us and parachutists floating almost overhead. We were frequently bombed, strafed and driven to earth by shrapnel and persistent dog-fighting.
>
> There was no peace at night either, and from the time we left our lodgings in the morning until our return in the evening, we were lucky if we had a piece of bread and cheese.
>
> After 18 days, the last aircraft was dismantled and dispatched, and we returned to 50 MU with several holes in the lorries, but no casualties. . . .

During the war the unit handled 12,000 aircraft, including the first intact Me110 to crash in England and Rudolf Hess's plane which, through some misunderstanding, was briefly displayed in St Giles' when it was meant to be 'Top Secret'.[11]

Much of the unusable wreckage brought to Cowley by No. 50 MU ended up at No. 1 MPRD which grew from quite small beginnings in the summer of 1940 to employ over 1,500 men and women and extend over 100 acres of farmland between Cowley and Horspath. With 8 miles of highways bearing names like Hurricane Road, Battle Road, Spitfire Road and Sunderland Road, it became 'a City of Wreckage where the oblong piles of debris were the fantastic houses, and the wing-tips poking their way out from the irregular roof-tops were the crazy, smokeless chimneys'. The extraordinary sight inspired the artist Paul Nash's painting *Totes Meer* (Dead Sea), a moonlit view of German aircraft heaped like breakers on a sandy shore. The two MPRDs – the other one was at Eaglescliffe near Stockton-on-Tees – reclaimed over 25,000 tons of high grade aluminium, sufficient for about 5,000 planes, by recycling wreckage and melting down the pans and other aluminium ware handed in by the public after Lord Beaverbrook's

Two Cowley employees complete the building of a Tiger Moth, the RAF's only primary trainer aircraft, c. 1942. The factory turned out forty of these planes every week.

appeal in July 1940. It also proved possible to save about 70,000 tons of other badly needed materials such as rubber, steel, non-ferrous metals, plastics and textiles.[12]

After inevitable dislocation at the outbreak of war, the formidable production capacity of the local Nuffield factories and Pressed Steel was completely harnessed to the war effort. Early in 1940 Morris Motors secured a contract to build the Tiger Moth, the RAF's primary training plane, and, despite the scepticism of traditional aircraft manufacturers, was soon turning out forty a week on the flow-line principle. The firm also manufactured 18 in and 21 in aerial and naval torpedoes by similar methods and other wartime products included wirelesses, seachlights, tail units for Horsa gliders, tripods for machine-guns and the power plants for Beaufighters and Lancaster bombers. From July 1940 Nuffield Exports undertook the assembly of an eventual 8,000 sea mines and sinkers; its lofty premises on the fringe of the Cowley complex also housed existing stocks of depth charges, beach mines and torpedoes which were brought in by special trains from vulnerable towns like Portsmouth and later dispersed to remote locations. In 1942 the building was reinforced and refitted for the manufacture of Crusader tanks and, with some difficulty, a workforce was assembled:

> There were college servants, farm hands, salesmen, butchers, bakers, and a few 'old lags'. There were Irishmen who always clung together and voiced their opinions in a body, and Welshmen whose leader was a short, stocky ex-miner who had once led a hunger march from the Rhondda Valley to Westminster. There was a Jew who had been for fifteen years a receptionist at an exclusive night-club in the West End of London, and who rose to the position of Planning Superintendent after taking a course of engineering at an Oxford night school. And then there was the Professor who took a keen interest in his work and became one of most skilful fitter-assemblers.[13]

Pressed Steel produced over 230,000 tons of steel and 27,000 tons of light alloys during the war and made nearly 2 million jerricans, 3½ million steel helmets, 1¼ million land mines and over 1 million frames for babies' gas masks. The number of employees regained pre-war levels during 1940, climbing from 6,785 in September 1940 to a peak of 8,820 in 1942. In addition, the Ministry of Supply built a large cartridge case factory at the northern end of the site in 1941 and this employed up to 887 people at its peak.[14]

Morris Radiators in North Oxford had produced an experimental radiator for the Spitfire just before the war, based on the 'secondary surface' radiator used in cars rather than the traditional 'honeycomb' design employed by aircraft manufacturers. The new radiator, using copper strip instead of solid copper tubes, was first tested in October 1939 and was an immediate success, entering large-scale production the following May. The factory also developed a coolant to prevent fuel from boiling at high altitudes and new cabin and gun heaters for aircraft; a new exhaust system for the Rolls-Royce Merlin engine prevented the flames from giving away the position of night-flying aircraft. Wartime output included radiators for Beaufighters, Lancasters and Mosquitoes, and other products such as ¼ million helmets, ½ million mess tins, thousands of field cookers and over a million boxes for 25-pounder shells. In these circumstances, the factory doubled in size and the workforce trebled to 3,000 people; at weekends, professionals – doctors, teachers and local government staff – lent a hand, but the firm expanded to Llanelli in 1945 because the local labour supply had been exhausted.[15]

The MG factory won a reconditioning contract early in 1940 and the growth of its repair and production work led to the enlargement of the press shops and expansion into the adjoining Pavlova leather works. Instead of sports cars, Crusader tanks and anti-aircraft Oerliken and Bofors tanks were assembled, and in the months before D-Day thousands of heavy tanks were converted for the use of engineers and sappers. Abingdon also produced the forward cabins of the fast Albemarle planes which dropped the first paratroops into Normandy and matched Cowley's output of outboard power units for the Lancaster bomber with the same number of inboard units. Other useful products included large quantities of ammunition storage bins, aircraft parts and blood transfusion accessories and literally thousands of sets of waterproofing equipment for tanks prior to the Normandy landings. The number of employees increased to 1,400 and

Now we've made 100; workers at the MG factory in Abingdon celebrate the completion of another forward cabin for the Albemarle plane in 1942.

Young and old played their part. Small boys were engaged straight from school for a job which no adult could do. These lads, holding a red-hot rivet, would have to squirm their way into a confined space within a tank, and there they would have to keep the rivet in position while a man outside drove it home with a ram to the accompaniment of a deafening splutter. Amid the drifting smoke and welding fumes, and above the ever-changing pattern of fiery sparks, sat placid-looking women in their lofty cranes, picking up and turning round 18 ton tanks with the expertness and delicacy of touch that ladies have at their fine needlework.[16]

The importance of the Northern Aluminium Company at Banbury was evident before the war and was stressed by Kingsley Wood, the Air Minister, when he visited the factory in May 1939:

Speed and promptitude in delivery in connection with the defence of the country is, I hardly need emphasise, of the utmost importance and value, and I am glad to know that this Company has been distinguished by the promptitude of their deliveries. . . . Here we have workpeople specially trained and skilled who are certainly doing their utmost in good team spirit to push on with our defence preparations.[17]

As well as continuing to produce aluminium alloy, the company's plants at Southam Road, Banbury and Adderbury also extruded airframes and wingspans, including thousands of wingspans for Lancaster bombers. Adderbury became a centre for the reprocessing of material from crashed aircraft and the firm's other products included aluminium powder for flares and incendiaries and landing strips for emergency airfields. In order to cope with the extra work, the NAC workforce trebled to 2,300 people, drawing in employees from miles around.[18] Other Banbury firms involved in wartime production included Spencer's, which made millions of igniter bags and repaired airmen's electronically heated gloves instead of manufacturing foundation garments, and the furniture makers Henry Stone & Son, who made tail units for Mosquitoes. The British Motor Boat Company made naval landing craft and inflatable dinghies and Switchgear & Equipment produced switchgear for military use, depth control gear for torpedoes and mine switches. O.K. Seal, a London firm which made milk bottle tops, relocated to Banbury in 1940 after its premises were destroyed in the Blitz and made parts for Vickers-Armstrong aircraft.[19]

Countywide, businesses large and small made their own significant contributions to the war effort. At Kingham the agricultural engineers Lainchbury & Sons Ltd began munitions work in October 1940, manufacturing parts for sea mines, rocket heads and bulkheads for magnetic mines.[20] Early's in Witney was used entirely for the manufacture of seamen's blankets, and J.H. Early was able to argue successfully that it was 'not unimportant to the Government, particularly the Admiralty' when the firm was threatened by the call-up of its Secretary/Accountant in 1943.[21] In Charlbury Dent's glove factory was taken over by De Havilland's and was used mainly for aircraft repair and re-covering fabric components.[22] As in the First World War, Lucy & Co.'s Eagle Ironworks turned to munitions work and manufactured shells, bombs, aircraft parts and mine sinkers at its premises in Walton Well Road, Oxford.[23] There was a continuing demand for the motor scythes and trenchers produced at Cowley by John Allen & Son's but during the winter of 1939/40 the firm produced prototypes of 'The Rabbit' and 'The Ferret', rather fantastical devices that were intended to breach the Germans' Siegfried Line. These weapons did not live up to expectations in tests, and development was abandoned after the fall of France. Instead, John Allen's went on to make machine-gun mountings, rocket-firing apparatus and parts for Bren gun carriers as well as hundreds of Sheepsfoot Rollers which were used in the construction of roads and airfields. Under conditions of secrecy, it produced a prototype flail which enabled tanks to cross minefields, only discovering the true purpose of the device after the battle of El Alamein. The firm's rolling and plant hire department was also very busy and helped to construct new aerodromes from the south coast to the Shetlands, including local airfields at Stanton Harcourt and Watchfield; another long-term contract was at Islip petroleum pumping station, the distribution centre for pipelines from Avonmouth and Southampton.[24]

Oxford University Press made a very different contribution to the war effort by publishing over seventy titles in a series of *Oxford Pamphlets on World Affairs*, which was designed to counter Nazi propaganda. About six million copies were sold and it has been said that they 'became as much a part of the wartime scene as gas masks and ration books'. The Press also printed huge numbers of highly

'The Rabbit', a prototype weapon produced by John Allen & Son which was designed to be launched against the Siegfried Line.

confidential papers, mostly Admiralty reports, for the Government, and John Johnson, the University Printer, felt compelled to stay there in case of air raids.[25] J.F. Fulton, an American visitor in October 1940, remarked that Johnson's

> fierce loyalty is positively frightening. He has not emerged from the Press for fourteen months. His cot is in his office and he has a barracks for fifteen men of the Press who also sleep in with him.[26]

If most war production took place in the adapted premises of older businesses, the policy of dispersing vital industry led to the building of a 'Hush-Hush' factory in Oxfordshire. The bombing of Nuffield Mechanizations' Coventry factory in November 1940 might have destroyed the firm's ability to manufacture the Bofors gun and the decision was taken to disperse the rifling machines to a well-concealed site in Tubney Wood, near Appleton. The first buildings were erected in the winter of 1940/1 and, 'whilst the bricks were being laid, pine trees that were very close to the building line were tied back with ropes to other trees and released to spring back when the walls were completed'; in addition, the roofs were slightly concave and conifers in large pots helped to perfect the camouflage. Production began in 1941, and by the middle of 1943 around 300 staff were working two twelve-hour shifts seven days a week and achieving a weekly output of about 200 Bofors gun barrels.[27]

Employees of the Crest Works at Stoke Row who were making parts for aeroplane engines. Some of the women have the letters C.W. embroidered on their overalls.

By no means all wartime production was undertaken by regular employees in established business premises. In Woodcote, for example, 'The Factory' operated at Wayside for most of the year under the direction of the Royal Army Ordnance Corps at Didcot; an average of twenty-five people attended for five hours every weekday and they were paid 1s 3¼d per hour to pack spares, make boxes and undertake cleaning and re-greasing work.[28] Labour shortages encouraged voluntary paid work, and in November 1943 fit men and youths were required to load ashes and clean locomotives at Oxford's Great Western Railway station, being offered normal rates of pay, overalls and the use of canteen and washing facilities.[29] Drifters, in Oxford at least, could always find some employment:

> If they were hungry there were plenty of stop-gap jobs – sorting scrap at the Cowley dump, humping sacks of flour at the food depots, assembling torpedoes at Pressed Steel, clerking in one of the Ministries that occupied every other quad, and, above all, firewatching.[30]

It was clearly essential to harness everyone's productive capacity and in July 1940, for instance, the Oxford Schools of Technology, Art and Commerce received a supply of materials for making small spare parts only twenty-four hours after the Board of Education had issued a memorandum about increasing the production of armaments.[31] In 1941 Oxford City Council was only able to justify building a new Engineering Block for the School of Technology on the grounds that the building and plant could be used by local firms for war production. Even schools were enlisted; when H.W.B. Joseph visited South

Oxford School in December 1941 he found boys in the woodwork centre making hammer and axe handles for Pressed Steel.[32]

Many businesses in the service sector discovered that war could provide new and lucrative markets. City Motors in Oxford won a three year contract from the Ministry of Supply to rebuild and overhaul damaged military vehicles, and the firm hired out used cars and trucks to the South Midland District of the Royal Army Supply Corps. With tyre rationing, it became the authorized tyre depot for the area, supplying both local needs and many large contractors. The Bicester branch became particularly busy following the establishment of the Ordnance Depot when vehicles were always in demand for building and maintenance work.[33] In April 1944 Henley Model Laundry was so overwhelmed with work for the British and American armed forces that it launched an advertising campaign with the slogan 'Is Your Bundle Really Necessary?' to try to limit its receipt of home laundry.[34] The Oxford drapers Cape & Co. secured an Air Ministry contract, possibly for black-out materials, and supplied over £5,000 worth of goods to local airfields and lesser amounts to other aerodromes in the south and the Midlands.[35] The Banbury photographer Norman Blinkhorn found many new areas of work as he told a local audience in 1943:

> One of the jobs which photographers were called on to do early in the war was to photograph legal and historic documents in case they were destroyed by enemy action. This was done by the making of minute negatives which could be enlarged to any size. . . . He then spoke of the airgraph service, and showed the audience a small spool capable of holding the negatives of one thousand letters. . . . Buildings of historic interest were also photographed for record purposes . . . and another unpleasant task they had to perform was that of photographing the bodies of unidentified air-raid victims. Photographers also acted as district censors of photographs, all these activities being in addition to their ordinary work, which itself provided plenty of interest, as shown by a photograph . . . of an egg laid locally, complete with the 'victory V sign'.[36]

The demands of essential war work and the absence of so many men on active service necessitated the large-scale employment of women, some of it in areas that would have been 'considered as quite unsuitable before the war'. At MG in Abingdon, for example, there was scope initially to recruit local farm labourers and then refugees from the bombing in London, but women eventually formed 40 per cent of the workforce.[37] The proportion of women employed at the Northern Aluminium Company in Banbury rose to 50 per cent and one woman from the Bartons later recalled her work in the packing and despatch department:

> After going through many processes and departments the sheets of metal came to us for packing. Lining the cases with paper we then oiled one side of a sheet and turned it over into the case so that the oil was next to the paper. As we did this every time there was always oil between each sheet and the last one was oiled on both sides. The paper was then folded over the top and wooden cleats nailed over this. Each cleat was then banded with a metal strip and a number stencilled on and, of course, an address. . . .
> After a month . . . I was made a packer, and had a mate of my own and so had

Women working with aluminium sheets at the Northern Aluminium Company's Banbury factory.

to work at a bench. During the day shifts we worked on the sheet metal, but on night shifts we worked on coils of metal. This was quite different and when we had oiled them they were wrapped in paper and then they had to be stacked. I must say it tested your muscles, as there was often sixty to seventy in a job of light metal, and your stack would be six or eight feet high when finished. Changes in the department put me on these coils for ten months. Some of the coils were of light metal but some were very heavy. One that I weighed was seventy-five pounds and there were twenty-six or so in a job. You can see one had to be quite fit to keep throwing these about. Our record shift was nearly nine tons for two women.[38]

Following an appeal from Ernest Bevin, the Minister of Labour, for more women munition workers early in 1941, fifty to sixty women came forward in Oxford and there was a campaign to encourage women undergraduates to do factory work in the vacations.[39] The numbers were still unequal to the task, however, and in September 1941 women shop assistants aged between twenty and twenty-five were called up for war work unless they worked in food departments. One of the young women affected spoke to an *Oxford Mail* reporter:

I don't mind being called up in the least, for I have no home ties. I shall hope to get into a factory, for I want to help produce something which will smash little Adolf and his gang.[40]

Among the new women workers at Cowley in the autumn of 1941 was 'Sally' Churchill – really Lady Sarah Spencer-Churchill, the eldest daughter of the

Duke and Duchess of Marlborough. She had volunteered for factory work in order 'to make a more vital contribution to the national effort', and her work at Morris Motors soon attracted attention:

> To her fellow workers she is popularly known as 'Sally', and she has won admiration with her gay, happy-go-lucky spirit, and the deep interest and industry which she displays in her job. . . . She has settled down quickly and happily, and is at present working a machine. Like many of her companions, she takes her mid-day meal in the works canteen, and often does not finish work until 7 p.m.[41]

The number of women working at Pressed Steel in Cowley rose from only 218 in 1938 to 2,435 in 1942, and more women than men were employed in the cartridge case factory.[42] Women were employed at John Allen & Son's from October 1941 both in the offices and in the manufacture of machine tools.[43] At De Havilland's in Witney,

> most of the women manual workers were engaged on stressed skin repairs, detail fittings, sheet metal and fabric work. Fabric workers were under the supervision of two skilled women from the parent factory and their work was the covering of wooden structures and components of De Havilland Queen Bees, Tiger Moths and Rapides with madapolin and fabric. This covering was

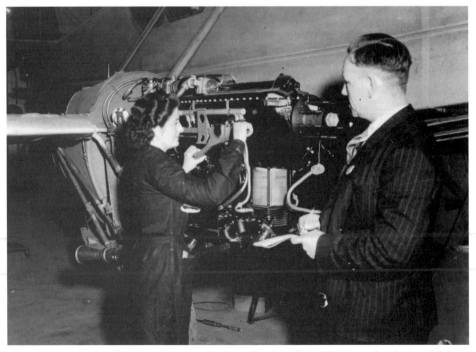

Miss Bailey instals a Gipsy engine at the De Havilland works in Witney under the watchful gaze of J.W. Baker, the Assistant Works Superintendent.

then coated with tautening 'dope'. Not surprisingly these girls were generally referred to as 'dope girls', although the high standard they achieved in their work disposed of any possible connotation the term could have with indulgence in sedatives or stimulants.[44]

In September 1942 an article in the *Oxford Mail* praised the ability of women from varying backgrounds to master the 'Stiffest Jobs' in the factory, and Morris Motors were advertising for women aged thirty-one or over because 'Work is held up owing to the shortage of labour'.[45] Women were also employed as sorters and postwomen by the Post Office, as drivers and conductresses by City of Oxford Motor Services Ltd, and as 'portresses' by the Great Western Railway Company.[46] Those with flying experience, including the renowned Amy Johnson, joined the Air Transport Auxiliary and ferried planes to and from Cowley, Witney and more distant airfields.[47]

The long days worked by many women posed new problems for employers and the authorities which had suddenly to consider child-care and other welfare provisions. At Cowley, Morris Motors provided a welfare officer and a clinic with trained nurses as well as facilities for indoor and outdoor recreation, but there had been no manifest need for a crèche for workers' children.[48] By November 1940, however, the Ministry of Labour felt that there were now so many women workers in Oxford that it was desirable to establish a day nursery in the city; furthermore, it agreed to pay 100 per cent of the cost of setting it up and a further sum of 1s a day per child accommodated.[49] Jesus College pavilion was requisitioned for the purpose and the crèche for the children of Cowley workers at the Crescent Road sports ground was the eighth in Oxford when it opened on 23 April 1942. Lord Nuffield performed the opening ceremony, lighting a candle for one-year-old birthday boy Bill Hare, and said that

> they all appreciated the part the women were playing in doing all they could to help beat that hound over the other side. It was up to everyone to look after the children while the women were at work. He thanked the employees for giving up the sports pavilion, which they did with the greatest pleasure. They would appreciate the good work that would be done there, and would have the satisfaction of knowing they had done all they could to help.[50]

Temporary premises in converted pavilions and other buildings were later supplemented by purpose-built day nurseries, such as those in Abingdon Road and Botley Road which were opened in 1943. By the end of that year there were places for over 500 children in Oxford.[51]

Similar facilities were provided by the County Council in towns such as Witney, Chipping Norton, Thame and Henley and in the villages of Littlemore and Great Milton. Outside Oxford, however, the population was inevitably more scattered and some councillors began to claim that the demand had been grossly exaggerated. At a Council meeting in July 1943, W. Tombs complained:

> some women, not war workers, were taking their children to day-nurseries so that they could stay at home 'gossiping at their front doors with their arms folded'.

Smiling faces at the wartime nursery in the Jesus College cricket pavilion in June 1941. This was one of many nurseries established in the city and county for the children of working mothers.

Attention was drawn to the cost per child each week which varied enormously from one nursery to another, ranging from an economical 10s 6d at Great Milton to as much as £2 7s 1d in Henley. The decision was taken not to open any more day nurseries,[52] and the Highfield Estate in Bicester never obtained the nursery hut which had first been proposed a year earlier; the equipment provided by the Ministry of Health was put into store until early 1944 when it was at last transferred to Wolverton Infants' School.[53]

One contemporary slogan argued that 'Ploughing on Farms is as Vital as Arms'[54] and efforts to increase war production in factories and workshops were paralleled by measures to maximize food production. The Oxfordshire War Agricultural Executive Committee was formed as a local arm of the Ministry of Agriculture and this body was empowered to take control of unproductive land and indeed badly managed farms, cultivating the land itself or encouraging others to do so.[55] At the Warren in Bradwell Grove, for example, the Committee organized the clearance of 45 acres of scrub and wasteland from November 1940 and this land was said to be producing some of the best wheat in the county by 1942.[56] More than 47 acres of Ewelme Common were brought into cultivation from 1941 and in 1944, 329 sacks of wheat and 250 tons of potatoes were harvested on it.[57] Golf-courses were robbed of their links in order to grow food, and in February 1943 it was reported that the Tadmarton course was entirely under the plough. Burford Golf Club had lost nine holes, North Oxford had

Land Girl Cynthia Durham poses with the farmer's granddaughter during a break from cleaning out the cowshed at Upper Copcourt Farm, Postcombe, in 1944.

surrendered a field and the Oxfordshire War Agricultural Executive Committee was asking Southfield Golf Club for a further 10 acres on top of the 78 that had already been taken.[58] At Henley in April 1944 holes 9, 10 and 11 were being used for grazing but the golf club had improvised an 11th hole to maintain a sixteen-hole course and provide weekend recreation for those engaged in urgent war work.[59]

In order to supervise farming throughout Oxfordshire, the executive committee divided the county into eight districts and one person was nominated from every two or three parishes to form each District Advisory Committee. Members of these district committees were in a good position to assess the agricultural potential of their localities and forwarded their recommendations to the parent body. Local farmers subsequently received orders which might require them to plough up areas of grassland, dictate which crops they were to grow and even specify how these were to be cultivated and manured. The system helped to increase food production by about 70 per cent in Benson and F.P. Chamberlain of Crowmarsh Battle Farm, a member of Bullingdon District Advisory Committee, reported proudly that in 1944 the parish had produced:

> 7,800 cwts wheat
> 10,300 cwts barley
> 2,500 cwts oats
> about 23,900 galls milk
> about 99,400 eggs
> 78 tons sugar beet
> and beef, mutton, bacon, honey, poultry[60]

The influence of War Agricultural Executive Committees over local farmers was strengthened in 1943 by the Farm Survey, which they carried out on behalf of the Ministry of Agriculture. This latter-day Domesday of farming practice examined each farm in detail and graded each farmer on a scale of A to C, the latter denoting marked inefficiency and warning the individual to improve or risk being replaced by another occupier. In Deddington R.W. Jeffery surveyed several farms in March 1943 and found that the Homestead, a 28¾ acre farm, was infested with charlock and couch grass. The farmer was branded as C because she was both ignorant and lazy. The farmer at Hempton also rated a C because of his 'lack of initiative and interest', and although the farmer at The Burge earned a B, he was condemned as a 'Poor manager on awkwardly situated farm' and his land was apparently full of 'charlock and poppys'.[61] Several farmers in the Benson area were reprimanded as a result of the survey, but nobody was dispossessed.[62]

Across the whole county the war threw into reverse the long-term trend away from arable, and between 1939 and 1944 the area under permanent grassland in Oxfordshire fell by 44 per cent from 251,000 acres to 140,000 acres; by contrast, the production of wheat, oats and, particularly, barley soared and the Ministry of Food built a rail-served grain silo at Kidlington in 1943 to resolve the problem of drying, storing and transporting the extra crops.[63] Most farmers probably saw these changes as being in the national interest and accepted the orders and rebukes of the War Agricultural Executive Committees as just another cross to bear. Their ability to do otherwise was, in any case, strictly limited and two farmers from the Ploughley district were fined £10 and £20 respectively in August 1940 after refusing to comply with orders to plough up grassland; in July Lord Faringdon was fined £40 because his agent at Buscot had failed to plough some land within the prescribed period.[64] William Mallett, a Bloxham smallholder, was fined £5 with costs in September 1941 after losing his temper with two officials from the Banbury Advisory Committee who wanted him to plough an extra 4½ acres. He argued that other farmers had enjoyed preferential treatment and called Richard Page a 'snotty-nosed little b——'; according to the other complainant, George Gibbard, he also threatened to 'swing for the pair of us', adding 'I reckon I should be doing as much good as if I were killing Germans'.[65]

The carrot as well as the stick was used to boost output and the Victory Churn contest, for example, encouraged dairy farmers to increase milk yields by giving Certificates of Merit to those who raised production by 10 per cent or 20 per cent. In 1943 the successful local farmers included J. French of College Farm, Deddington, Raymond Good of Sydenham Grange and W.S. Rogers of Manor Farm, Bletchington, who was particularly commended.[66]

The human resources of the farming community were stretched to the limit by the need for greatly increased production at a time when farm labourers were joining the armed forces or opting for better paid war work in the factories. Mechanization provided one possible solution to the crisis and

Early in 1943 there was great excitement at Crowmarsh Battle Farm when the Massey-Harris Combine Harvester arrived in pieces from Canada and the hands turned out to help the Firm's mechanic to assemble it.

A second combine was acquired in 1945, achieving huge savings of time and labour but, as F.P. Chamberlain recorded in 1942, it was exceptionally difficult to obtain farm machinery in wartime:

The price of new Implements has gone up 50 per cent to 100 per cent. To get one, the procedure is: go to your merchant: he makes contact with maker: maker says OK: then fill in Form & send it to the War Agri. Comee.: WAC sends it to the District Adviser: DA says the machine is necessary for the proper cultivation of the land: the chit is sent back round to the buyer: who can then order the machine: maker says that if he can get the material: it may be sent off sometime: usually not under 6 months, often a year or more: because your name is someway down the list.[67]

In wartime conditions it generally proved more practicable to supplement the agricultural workforce by using Land Girls, soldiers, prisoners of war and volunteers. The Government had decided to recruit a Women's Land Army in April 1939 and thousands of young women, many of them from an urban background, were encouraged to volunteer by the patriotic slogan 'That Men May Fight' or the more prosaic 'Ballet Dancers Can Drive Tractors'.[68] Some received preparatory training courses and Jean Cordrey, for example, spent four weeks at Shipton Court before being sent to work for Mr Stops at Manor Farm, Alkerton, in September 1940; at Long Wittenham in 1939 twenty-five to thirty women every fortnight were being trained as tractor drivers at the Institute for

Women's Land Army float outside Henley Town Hall on Farm Sunday in June 1943. The place-name on the war memorial had been obliterated in 1940 to confuse the enemy in the event of an invasion.

Research in Agricultural Engineering.[69] The instruction was not always adequate and Norah Watts from Salford and another Land Girl found their training farm to be a smallholding where they were left hopelessly struggling for an hour to milk the two cows.[70] For some there was no prior training at all, and Mrs Bradshaw, coming from the confectionery business to the Women's Land Army, was sent straight to a hostel at Westcott Barton Manor and simply 'watched what others did in the fields'.[71]

The Land Girls, in their smart khaki breeches and green pullovers, were at first regarded with considerable scepticism, and farmworkers around Burford referred to them scathingly as 'They Wimmen' or 'Them Wenches'.[72] Such prejudices were only strengthened when, for example, an ex-waitress cycled several miles in a downpour to complain to her supervisor that her employer had left her alone in a field all morning 'where anything might have happened to her'.[73] In another case, a Land Girl was understandably shocked by her first experience of pig-killing:

> He'd asked me to make the bed of straw, which I did and the two men got the pig out which you can imagine was absolutely screaming like anything. Cowman had said, 'do you want to hold its hind quarters?'. I said, 'no, not on your life – I'll hold its head', and I held its head until I saw what the farmer was going to do. I hadn't realized that he was going to stick the pig with the knife and I squealed then as loud as the pig and I let go of the pig. You can imagine what happened then; the pig ran away and they had to catch it again. . . .[74]

Farmworkers in Fifield 'set up' Doree Griffin by getting her to harness the huge shire horse[75] and many Land Girls had a mixed reception from their employers. Marjorie Batstone recalled that some local farmers were very good but

> there were some real beasts – used to treat us as if we were, well, like the cows in the field, but we didn't get very many like that. There was a few round the Oxfordshire area that was really rather awful to work for, but we just had to put up with it.[76]

The farmer employing Doree Griffin and others at Hill Farm, Fifield, certainly made few concessions:

> We were unloading cwt sacks of potatoes from a big wagon which had come in the barn. And we had to carry these sacks up the tallest steps up into a barn, just us girls doing it and 1 cwt sack of potatoes isn't very easy, you get it across your shoulders to carry it up these steps. Well, the farmer happened to walk by with some of his weekend visitors from town, they were watching us and I overheard one of them say to him 'Isn't that rather hard work for a girl?' 'Huh! That's what I pay them for.'[77]

In spite of the early doubts, many farmers became very appreciative of the Land Girls' work, and at one stage there were as many as 1,700 of them employed on Oxfordshire farms.[78] Their hours were long and Marjorie Batstone remembered leaving the Cokethorpe hostel soon after 7 a.m., returning at 5.30 to

6 p.m. in winter or as late as 10 p.m. in the summer. She helped with general farm work – ploughing, haymaking, harvesting and hedge-cutting; another Land Girl, June Young, also undertook a wide variety of tasks while she was based at Hall Place hostel in Sparsholt:

> Strawberry picking, they taught us how to make crate boxes . . . , they taught us how to make cabbage nets, they wouldn't let us be idle; even snow digging one winter, we was all snowed in one winter . . . and they sent us out, we had to clear the roads snow digging. Did strawberry picking at the other side of Kingston Bagpuize. Harvesting, every aspect you were roped into for harvesting, from cutting and stooking the sheaves, pitching it into the wagons then placing your life in your hands you'd take it out of there and disgorge it into the elevator to go on to this rick.

Other Land Girls specialized in dairy work, helped to run market gardens or joined the timber corps.[79]

Soldiers and, later in the war, prisoners of war provided additional manpower in the countryside. Engineers from the Bailey Bridging camp at Howbery Park occupied spare summer evenings by helping to clear Ewelme Common for cultivation, and soldiers also assisted with the clearance of the Warren at Bradwell Grove.[80] Italian prisoners of war were extensively used in Oxfordshire, and by the end of March 1942 they were said to have put in 40,433 man hours on various land drainage schemes. There followed a lengthy dispute when the authorities

Soldiers help to gather in the harvest at Fawley Bottom near Henley in August 1941.

tried to charge 1s per man-hour for this work, but they eventually agreed that Oxfordshire County Council would pay between 1.384d and 7.25d per man-hour according to the standard of work achieved on each scheme. Writing to the Divisional Engineer of the Thames Conservancy about the Haseley Land Drainage Scheme in March 1942, Arnold Forster commented:

> Mr Stanley Hawkin, the farmer chiefly concerned, told me that he estimated the value of the work being done by the Prisoners at about 5 pence per hour, judging by the time it would take an ordinary farm labourer to do the same work at present rates of wages.[81]

Land Girls worked with Italian POWs at Duns Tew farm, and at Hill Farm in Fifield, as Doree Griffin recalled:

> Italian POWs were brought into this farm every day. Their work was mainly ditching. We noticed that their equipment was far superior to ours. We had a terrible job to get replacements for wellingtons, gum boots as we called them, because of the shortage of rubber; them Italians had beautiful things, right up to their thighs, to do their ditching. They also had allocation of oil to cook their chips and food. We could smell this gorgeous smell coming from the hedgerow where the Italian cook was preparing their meal. And also if it was pouring with rain they left us poor girls out in the field muck spreading, we stuck it all day long in the pouring rain; these (Italians) were under the hedge sheltering from the rain until their lorry came to take them home.[82]

Towards the end of the war Italian, Latvian, Lithuanian and German POWs were working on farms around Westwell[83] and it was claimed that the generous provision of POW labour was responsible for making potatoes the most important root crop grown in wartime Oxfordshire.[84]

At harvest time particularly, volunteers were a crucial source of labour on farms. In July 1940, for instance, over 200 volunteers, more than half of them from Oxford University, responded to an appeal from the Oxfordshire War Agricultural Executive Committee and helped to bring in the local harvest. In just two months the committee had placed seventy-five volunteers with farmers and Oxfordshire County Council had also released ninety-three roadmen to work on farms.[85] During the summer term that year senior boys from Bicester School were released early on three afternoons a week to help local farmers.[86] Schoolchildren were also encouraged by a Government campaign to undertake war work in the holidays, and in August 1940 boys from the City of Oxford High School, Southfield School and Magdalen College School took part in a Schools Forestry Camp where 1,224 tons of pit-props were cut in just eight weeks. In 1942 a party of about 100 boys from the City of Oxford High School attended harvest camps:

> They harvested corn, potatoes and fruit. They contended with thistles, nettles, brambles and wasps. They harvested in the hottest days of the year; and some boys were soaked to the skin with rain two or three times in the course of a working day. There were compensations, however; the work was of national

importance and the farmers were grateful for our help; food was plentiful and much appreciated; there was 'time off' at weekends, and there was the satisfaction of earning one's keep by doing a man's job.[87]

At Bignell Park Evacuated School near Bicester the school closed for a fortnight's Potato Harvest Holiday in the autumn of 1944, and even after this the headmaster noted that, on 26 October, eleven boys had been 'exempted for potato picking today'.[88] Children at Milton and Shipton-under-Wychwood also went out in gangs to lift potatoes and their teachers organized competitions to destroy pests such as Cabbage White butterflies.[89]

Agricultural holiday camps for adults were being established in Oxfordshire in June 1943, and these included men's camps at Banbury and Chipping Norton and a women's camp at Bletchington. Volunteers undertook to work at least one thirty-hour week and were charged £1 2s 6d a week for their food and accommodation; men received 1s an hour for their labour and women 10d.[90]

The Ministry of Agriculture's 'Dig for Victory' campaign did much to stimulate food production in towns and villages. By October 1939 boys at Didcot Senior School were digging up part of their playing field for allotments, and at the City of Oxford High School for Boys

some twenty-five boys have taken allotments on the School field (avoiding however the sacred turf of the 1st XI pitch) and are busy digging for victory in their spare time. In spite of initial difficulties of hard ground and nettle roots the school allotments have produced some excellent crops.[91]

Wantage Council School planted 5 cwt of potatoes and 4,000 brassicas on allotments which it cultivated on the Springfield Road site for a new senior school.[92] Gosford Hill School in Kidlington cultivated an extensive garden during the first year of the war. An *Oxford Mail* reporter noted:

When I visited the school gardens recently, I was impressed by 50 rows of swedes. In fact, there was an entire plot of swedes. There were at least eight different kinds of brassica. There were also some very healthy crops of various kinds of root vegetables. . . . Fruit trees are plentiful and the girls of the school have made 96 lb of jam from the black currants. Damsons have been bottled and chutneys have been made. Bees and a goat are among the livestock kept, and the goat is the great pet of the London evacuees.

By November 1940 the County's Horticultural Adviser was able to report that 2,392 children, excluding evacuees, were having gardening lessons and that 30 acres were now under cultivation by Oxfordshire schools.[93] In Oxford Mrs M.D. Lobel, a sub-librarian at the Bodleian Library, set up the Co-operative War Allotments Corps in the summer of 1940 to involve schoolchildren, scouts and guides in the 'Dig for Victory' campaign. The gardeners wore green armlets bearing the letters CWAC and their produce was destined for local hospitals.[94]

Many more allotments were provided in urban areas, and by the time that Freddy Grisewood launched Oxford's 'Dig for Victory' week in January 1942 the number of ten-pole allotments in the city had risen from a pre-war figure of 3,986 to 5,880; the cultivated area had grown by 81 per cent from 248 acres to 448 acres.[95] These new allotments utilized, for example, the site of a proposed branch library at New Marston and areas of Bury Knowle, Cutteslowe and Raleigh Parks.[96] The City Council was frustrated in its desire to cultivate South Park by restrictive covenants, but the University released some land for allotments in the University Parks and even the tiny space outside the Examination Schools in Merton Street was used to grow a few vegetables.[97] In October 1940 the *Oxford Mail* reported that Mr Witham of East Oxford had raised a crop of onions worth ten guineas on Southfield allotments from seeds that had cost only 9s.[98] In 1943 local allotment holders were further encouraged by the receipt of 1,000 boxes of seeds from the British War Relief Society in New York.[99]

'Dig for Victory' leaflets urged every gardener to grow fruit and vegetables and many private gardens exchanged their peacetime verdure for fruit bushes and rows of vegetables. Oxford council house tenants were encouraged to grow vegetables by the prospect of up to 200 grants of 5s.[100] At Benson Mrs Ethel Miller's 1 acre garden was put into 'battle-dress' and sales of produce raised £317 4s 6d for the RAF Benevolent Fund. The gardener, H.J. Winfield, recalled:

> Those unnecessary flower beds were dug up, flowers became a luxury, and in their places went lettuces, onions, cabbage, and all the other useful crops that the housewife can make so much of. Decks were stripped for action, and the garden responded as a well-worked garden will. There is always a sad look about a garden without flowers, but so there is about a lady with a fur coat and ladders in her stockings! Both look wrong, but I believe that both did their duty![101]

The Village Produce Association encouraged communities to make themselves self-sufficient and to sell communally grown food to the best advantage. The people of Somerton started a branch in 1943 after calling in the expertise of the Ministry of Agriculture to resolve the problem of Mrs Butler's voracious pig. Provided with technical advice, supplies bought in bulk and shared tools, the villagers established sections for rearing rabbits, pigs and poultry and set up new allotments. A village stall was opened in the summer to sell the food which virtually everyone, young and old, had helped to produce.[102]

The Oxfordshire Federation of Women's Institutes established an Oxfordshire Garden Produce Committee which encouraged food production by distributing 4,200 soft fruit bushes to members and organizing the collection and sale of produce.[103] As part of a nationwide campaign, the local federation also created a network of fifteen Fruit Preservation Centres across the county, one of which was based in the Council School at Charlbury.[104] The centres were an enormous success, and in March 1942 Lady Tweedsmuir, the President of the Oxfordshire Federation, wrote to each one thanking members for their work in the previous year:

> Over ten tons of jam were made in Oxfordshire, in addition to canned and bottled fruit, pickles and chutney, and fruit syrup. The whole of England produced enough jam to supply a quarter of a million people with their jam rations for a year. This in spite of an exceptionally bad fruit season. . . .

Women from the Hanney Co-operative Fruit Preservation Centre use an old farm wagon to celebrate their achievements in 1945.

Warning has been given that the food situation will be more difficult next winter. The fruit crop may be heavy and it is most essential that no fruit should be wasted. Oxfordshire will, I feel certain, play its part.[105]

If food production provided such a vital focus for voluntary effort, schools, local organizations and private individuals found numerous other ways of supporting the war effort. In September 1940, for instance, pupils at Oxford Central Girls' School were keeping local hospitals supplied with flowers.[106] Country schools were urged by the Board of Education to collect sheep's wool from the hedgerows and send it to the appropriately named Gathered Wool Officer at Bradford; they were also encouraged to gather acorns, beechmast, chestnuts, dandelions and the roots of autumn crocuses.[107] Children at Albury and Tiddington School despatched 81 lb of sheep's wool in April 1942 and collected 3 cwt of horse chestnuts in the autumn, sending them off to be made into glucose by Mcleans, manufacturing chemists.[108] More than 15 tons of rosehips were picked for their Vitamin C content in Oxfordshire and Buckinghamshire in 1943, and volunteers in the Banbury area forwarded 250 lb of foxglove leaves and 126 lb of raspberry leaves to be dried.[109] Much of this material probably went to the Oxford Medicinal Plants Scheme, a minor industry which was developing at Islip, where plants with a medicinal value were grown and dried.[110]

Voluntary organizations undertook a huge range of wartime tasks. Founded in 1938 the Women's Voluntary Service had 280 village organizers in Oxfordshire by the end of 1940 and members 'had to be adaptable and elastic in mind and in body, to be ready to turn from wrestling with household "chores" to any one of the innumerable problems that were to come upon us'. Asked what WVS stood for, a young London evacuee summarized them as 'The bloomin' women wot works for nuffin'. In Charlbury their multifarious work included

> regular hours of duty every week at the British Restaurant (1942–5), helping to give out new ration books and identity cards, the weekly sale of meat pies to agricultural workers, assistance at a Welcome Club for American soldiers, the supply of flowers and a team of visitor-helpers twice a week to the American Red Cross at the 317th American General Hospital at Ramsden Heath, salvage collecting and knitting for the Forces and for children of liberated Europe.[111]

At Binfield Heath Mrs Whiteley, as the local representative, directed the work of over 250 knitters who made 4,275 garments for the armed forces and the merchant navy.[112] Burford Women's Institute missed only one of its regular monthly meetings throughout the war and

> Our members took their full share in all the wartime activities of Burford, as well as running some of their very own such as collecting waste paper, jam-making, holding a potato bar in response to the urging by the Government to use more potatoes, the cultivation of a communal allotment and the organization of a produce stall in the High Street.[113]

The YMCA ran a popular canteen at the Red Triangle Club in Charlbury from October 1940 and the village also boasted a Red Cross working party which produced 2,175 garments for hospitals, children and the forces between October 1939 and August 1945.[114] At Leafield local members of the Voluntary Car Pool organization took patients to hospital and provided emergency transport when needed.[115]

Much voluntary work arose out of personal initiatives, and in July 1940, for example, Mrs Sweatman of Chalfont Road, Oxford, encouraged about thirty of her friends to meet weekly at St Giles' Parish Room

> to darn the socks, sew on buttons, repair clothing and do alterations where they are needed for any soldier, sailor or airman who cares to send a garment along.[116]

Mrs Marie Beazley, wife of the Lincoln Professor of Archaeology, personally organized a team of fifty-eight volunteers to knit an ingenious garment which she named the 'Kredemnon' after a garment worn by Ulysses. It was a woollen cylinder which servicemen could wear in seven different ways:

1. Stick your head into the cylinder: it will keep you warm and won't blow away.
2. Turn it down and make a stiff double collar of it.
3. Pull one edge over your head, and the other over your shoulder; and stuff the loose part in front into the cylinder.

4. If you don't want it up to your eyes, roll it back from the face.
5. Make a turban of it.
6. Get into it and wear it round your body to protect your middle and back. (But get in feet first, so as not to stretch it too much.)
7. Make a skirt of it while your clothes are drying.

In spite of its appearance, the 'Kredemnon' was well received and a knitting pattern was published with the more prosaic name 'The Greenock Multiwrap', to encourage its wider distribution.[117]

Voluntary effort helped to increase the number of village libraries in the county from 230 in 1939 to 312 in 1942, thereby providing a service to schools, RAF stations and Women's Land Army hostels.[118] Fifty-one people attended the first blood donor session in Benson in August 1943 and forty-eight Leafield residents volunteered as blood donors during the war.[119] Even pigeon fanciers across the county became part of the war machine by supplying hundreds of birds to the Army Pigeon Service of the Royal Corps of Signals. Between 1941 and 1943 pigeons were used to fly messages around the country when air raids hindered normal communication; after D-Day, local birds also carried vital pictures of flying-bomb sites.[120] The sheer scale and variety of voluntary effort was perhaps best summarized by 82-year-old Mary Miles of Islip:

My Voluntary Contributions through the six years of war.

I bileted two vacuees.
I knitted scarfs, socks, and pullovers for the Navy.
I mended, darned, and patched vest, pants, and pullovers, and darned socks, for soldiers.
I helped with the drying of Medical herbs in Dr James drying sheds.
I attended make mend and do classes.
I joined the WVS, attended every lecture on first aid and how to use the strup pump, and learn the diferent type of poison gas.
I sold Meat Pies to the agriculture workers.
and grew all my own vegetables and Soft Fruits.[121]

There was, finally, a significant area of work that was associated with Oxford University. In March 1945 Harry Plowman, Town Clerk of Oxford, remarked that

the University and colleges have functioned much more normally than was the case in the last war . . . most of the men's colleges have been able to continue to function through the provision of short-term courses for service cadets.[122]

Richard Burton was one such person, enrolling at Exeter College in April 1944 for a six-month course which combined English with intensive training for the RAF. J.R.R. Tolkien, Professor of Anglo-Saxon at Oxford, had to organize a new syllabus for cadets in the English School, and modified many of his lectures to suit a less specialized audience. In general terms, however, his life was much as it had been before the war and he wrote to his son, Michael, in January 1941 stating that 'life has been rather dull, and much too full of committees and legislative business, which has kept me up late several nights . . .'.[123]

Some of the women of the Binfield Heath Knitting Circle who made a total of 4,275 garments during the war.

The Bodleian Library remained open throughout the war, albeit with less than half of its peacetime staff, and it was the only national library to do so. At the Radcliffe Science Library opening hours had to be extended because of the amount of research being carried out there for the Government. The New Bodleian Library housed the British Red Cross and the regional offices of the Blood Transfusion Sevice and the Royal Observer Corps; it also accommodated the Royal National War Libraries, the Educational Books Section of the Prisoner of War Department and the naval intelligence departments of the Admiralty.[124] The voluntary blood transfusion service was established at the Bodleian in July 1940, and in its first three years attracted 3,000 donors to 323 sessions. Blood products were initially sent to the Radcliffe Infirmary on an ice-cream vendor's bicycle, but the service was soon providing about 3,000 bottles a year, meeting the entire needs of the Radcliffe and the Wingfield-Morris Hospital and also supporting the work of the Churchill Hospital.[125] In its role as Oxford Group Centre for the Royal Observer Corps, the Bodleian Library was the clearing house for information about local aircraft movements which were phoned through by local observers, plotted on a gridded map table and then forwarded to Headquarters, Fighter Command at Stanmore in Middlesex.[126] The Prisoner of War Department took the Bodleian and Oxford into the remotest theatres of war; in 1943, for example, Sub-Lieutenant R.F. Morgan, an old boy of the City of Oxford High School for Boys, told the school magazine that he had just received Maths, Science, French and Mapping text books from the Bodleian at a Vichy France internment camp in the Sahara Desert.[127] Earlier, Oflag V11 in Germany had become the first POW camp to establish a university, providing a series of lectures which were supported by books from Oxford.[128] The naval intelligence presence at the New Bodleian Library meant that the reading room played a part in formulating plans for the D-Day landings.[129]

For humanity, the most significant work in wartime Oxford was the medical research into the use of penicillin which Howard Florey and his colleagues undertook at the Sir William Dunn School of Pathology. After two years of research penicillin was first tested on a human being at the Radcliffe Infirmary on 17 January 1941. The patient, who is thought to have been an Oxford woman named Elva Akers, developed a fever but this reaction was soon attributed to the presence of a toxin which could be removed by further purification. Florey felt that the way was now clear to treat a severe case of bacterial infection and the age of antibiotics was launched on 12 February when Albert Alexander, a desperately ill Berkshire policeman, was given intravenous injections of penicillin. The initial results were remarkable, but supplies of the drug soon began to run out:

> Each time Alexander passed urine into a bottle it was unclipped and the member of the team in attendance at the bedside would cycle through the streets of Oxford, with the bottle of urine, back to the laboratory where Chain, Abraham or Heatley would re-extract the penicillin for re-injection into the constable's veins. Ethel, Sanders, Fletcher and others were all couriers in what some people grimly called the 'P-patrol'.

Despite these efforts, the penicillin supply was exhausted by the fifth day and, attacked by fresh infection, the patient had a relapse and died on 15 March. By

June 1941 a further five tests had conclusively proved the value of pure penicillin and it was only necessary to ensure the production of sufficient quantities. This could not be done in wartime Britain, and later in the year Florey went to the United States with his colleague, Dr Norman Heatley. American drug companies were persuaded to take up the challenge and subsequent war casualties, as well as countless civilians, benefited from research which had been pioneered in Oxford.[130]

In Oxfordshire, as elsewhere, war work generally meant long working hours interspersed with moments of light relief. Almost every day women at the Northern Aluminium Company in Banbury gathered round the canteen piano for a brief sing-song and

> we used to play up at times when there wasn't much work to do, dancing and talking in odd corners till the charge-hand came on the scene. Then we would each clean our lockers out and make everything in the department clean and tidy as compensation for being idle. Then there was the excitement of holidays and Christmas time. I remember one girl had a piece of mistletoe and gave the charge-hand a resounding kiss, which, although he was a married man, made him blush, and we saw no more of him for quite a long time.

Such incidents enlivened hours of heavy work but, going home off the night shifts, nearly all the women would fall asleep on the bus, 'nodding their heads one against the other, some with their mouths open, and even falling off the seats'.[131]

CHAPTER SEVEN

Savings and Salvage

Savings and salvage campaigns set out to engage the entire population in the war effort with slogans such as 'Hit Back with National Savings', 'Lend, Don't Spend', 'Kill the Squander Bug' and 'Saucepans into Spitfires'. The success of these campaigns was to be judged not only in terms of the money raised or the war materials supplied but also by their contribution to improved civilian morale and greater community spirit.

From the first, individuals everywhere were urged to buy defence bonds, National Savings certificates and savings stamps from local post offices. In

Mrs Scott, the village schoolmistress, pays in the week's savings at Lewknor post office.

January 1940 Banbury opened its own enquiry bureau to encourage public support for the National Savings movement and the mayor launched the proceedings by buying 500 savings certificates.[1] By March local investment in Government War Stock had reached £100,000 and a 'thermometer' was fixed to the Town Hall to monitor the town's progress. The Banbury National Savings Committee set a target of £500,000 in June and more than 100 streets in the town eventually had their own savings groups.[2] Between November 1939 and June 1940 National Savings in Oxford raised just over £1 million, and the General Post Office Savings Bank report for 1940 confirmed the city, with savings of £771,580, as the top saver among places with a population of between 50,000 and 100,000. A giant savings thermometer was unveiled at Carfax Tower and, like the one in Banbury, it served both to remind and encourage passers-by.[3] Smaller communities were no less keen to do their bit and Burford and Fulbrook, for example, raised about £1,300 in small continuous savings during the war;[4] in March 1941 Kennington Parish Council announced that 395 people, out of a population of 1,200, had their names on savings sheets, and that £4,036 5s worth of savings certificates had been sold.[5] Factories and schools were also coming together to form National Savings groups and the Northern Aluminium Company published a special edition of its employee magazine in July 1940 to introduce a scheme in its Banbury factory.[6] In the same month the works canteen at Morris Motors was crowded when Lord Nuffield drew out the prize-winning ticket in a £1,000 National Savings ballot.[7] Children were involved by school campaigns, and during 1940 Summertown School raised £154 9s in war savings.[8]

The success of Lord Beaverbrook's Spitfire Fund in 1940 led to an annual series of war savings weeks in which donors were encouraged to believe that their

Two boys, Colin Collis (left) and Colin Turner, dress up as bride and groom in a fancy dress competition as part of a war savings drive in Stoke Row.

money was being used for a specific purpose. Oxford opened its Fighter Fund in
June 1940, aiming to raise the £5,000 that was required to buy a single Spitfire.
Lord Nuffield promised to give a cheque equal to the highest individual
contribution and the fund eventually reached £7,618 14s 4d.[9] Similar appeals
were launched in Banbury and Chipping Norton later in the year and a shot-
down Messerschmitt fighter was exhibited in both towns in December to
stimulate interest and donations.[10] Faringdon's Fighter Fund began in August
1940 with the optimistic couplet,

> The RAF will fly the Spitfire,
> Let our District be the Buyer.[11]

Smaller towns were unable to raise the whole cost of a Spitfire, but still made
valuable contributions. The *Faringdon Advertiser* recorded in September how the
local campaign attracted huge public interest on its way to a final sum of £1,433
0s 3d:

Gifts to the 'Spitfire' continue to come in and at the time these notes were
written a live calf had been promised by a local farmer; on Monday afternoon, a
live bantam hen arrived together with the corn to feed her. A little boy, not yet
four, came in with a tiny gun, one of his treasures, and said solemnly 'This is to

*The Spitfire purchased for the RAF with the money raised by the City of Oxford Fighter Fund
in 1940.*

kill Hitler with'. His sister, a little older, brought also her greatest treasure, her sewing and embroidery box, all fitted with silks and cottons. Two tiny children from Woolstone have sent 3*d* each, which has been handed over to the Central Fund.[12]

A War Weapons Week was held in major population centres at the beginning of December 1940 and Oxford planned to raise £500,000, the cost of twenty-five bombers. Members of the public happily paid 6*d* to inspect a Junkers Ju88 bomber which had recently been brought down near Blewbury, and the fund was swollen by large donations from Lord Nuffield and Pressed Steel and from the University and colleges. The city therefore amassed £1,208,268 and benefited from the inevitable comparison with Cambridge which raised only £813,532.[13] War Weapons Weeks were held elsewhere in the county during September 1941, and the Chipping Norton and Woodstock districts exceeded their target of £150,000 by just over £100,000.[14] At Islip an ingenious barometer encouraged local people to raise much more than the target figure of £4,000:

> An effigy of Hitler is seen hanging from the gibbet at the top of the barometer and as the target is reached Hitler drops into the Hell-fire among the demons below. The barometer bears the words: 'Help to Roast Hitler'.[15]

The established formula was used again to stage a Warship Week in 1941–2, Wings for Victory Week in 1943, Salute the Soldier Week in 1944 and a Thanksgiving Week in 1945. Fritwell managed to raise £12,656 for Wings for Victory Week, an astonishing average of £25 per person.[16] Hook Norton's Warship Week achieved twice its projected income of £4,000 and Harpsden did equally well during Salute the Soldier Week in 1944:

> With their target fixed at £3,000 the people of Harpsden watched with interest the finger of the life-size model soldier outside the Village Hall creep up the indicator and pass this figure on Thursday and finally rest at £6,100 14*s* for the week. The target was therefore more than doubled, and they will be able to buy their soldiers not one, but two armoured cars.[17]

The very different communities of Oxford, Burford and the Bartons exceeded their targets in all of the special savings weeks and Burford held an additional Aircraft Week in August 1942 which raised £24,800.[18] Oxford also collected £444,988 in a Tanks for Attack campaign during October 1942 and smaller sums for the Merchant Navy Comforts Service and Airborne Forces Security Fund in 1943–4.[19] With a population of 150,000, Banbury and District raised more than £3 million pounds between November 1939 and June 1943.[20] A whole host of other savings campaigns tempted the patriotic citizen and, as an evacuee to Burford recalled,

> Flag days became a regular, sometimes a weekly happening, and we began to wonder how we could go on asking the same people time after time. But there was nothing to fear as we were always met with a smile and given a willing contribution. Indeed, it became quite amusing to see how many people kept their flags and tried to see how many they could collect.[21]

A recently shot down Junkers Ju88 bomber is displayed in St Giles', Oxford, as a fund-raising attraction during War Weapons Week in December 1940. The Mayor, Alderman C.J.V. Bellamy (right), is an early visitor.

There was extensive fund-raising to provide comforts for soldiers and prisoners of war and in Benson, for instance, the Women's Institute sent 2s 6d as a Christmas gift to each serving Bensonian in 1941 and 1942; the local branch of the British Legion added a further 5s, having raised most of this money through a series of dances and entertainments at the village hall.[22] At the Northern Aluminium Company the Services Comforts Fund regularly sent postal orders worth 7s 6d to employees in the services and 6s 6d to their wives; it also sent parcels to prisoners of war through the Red Cross.[23] In November 1941 the Honorary Secretary of the Welfare and Comforts Fund at Cowley Barracks appealed for 'godfathers' and 'godmothers' to provide extra support for children whose fathers had gone missing or were prisoners of war.[24] A Thame Prisoner of War Fund was supplying seventeen prisoners with a regular supply of cigarettes in November 1942[25], and in February 1944 Henley Home Guard Entertainments Committee raised £650 19s 5d for the Henley Prisoners of War Fund by holding a dance at the Town Hall.[26] In the autumn of 1940 Ald. C.J.V. Bellamy launched the Mayor of Oxford's Air Raid Distress Fund to provide money, clothes and furniture for victims of the Blitz who had been evacuated to Oxford; in June 1941 Mrs Elizabeth Pakenham sent the mayor a rather unusual contribution to this fund:

Please accept enclosed cheque for £17 13s 10d for your fund for air-raid victims. It may interest you to know that the money was raised by stripping off the gold braid from the uniform of the late Earl of Longford, my husband's

Marching past the saluting base at Chipping Norton during War Weapons Week in September 1941. The combined Chipping Norton and Woodstock districts raised £250,188 through the week's events.

father, who commanded the Oxfordshire Yeomanry (though this particular gold braid, that has been melted down, came off his Life Guard's uniform!)[27]

Small regular sums were collected, in Charlbury and Wootton among other places, for the Red Cross Penny-a-Week Fund.[28] Later in the war the Duchess of Marlborough tried to boost this modest form of saving by awarding a Rural Pennies Shield to the village which collected the largest sum in proportion to its population; the winner announced in February 1944 was Tiddington, with Nettlebed and the Bartons in joint second place.[29] There was always a place, too, for the kind of enterprise shown by Silvia Greany and Dorli Schulz, two youngsters who collected 7s 6d for the Red Cross in Oxford by cleaning cars, bicycles and shoes in the Jack Straw's Lane area.[30]

Salvage offered many further opportunities for individual and community involvement in the war effort. A government circular appealing for salvage was issued at the beginning of 1940, and local authorities were allocated the task of collection and distribution. Oxford householders were urged to send their waste paper to a central depot in February 1940, and two months later the mayor began a city-wide salvage campaign with the slogan, 'It's a Waste to Waste Waste'.[31] At the same time, Banbury's Borough Surveyor, Sidney Hilton, launched a new drive in municipal salvage:

The much despised dustbin now assumes national importance. Hitherto regarded as a dump for unwanted rubbish, it now becomes the receptacle for potential war resources.[32]

Buglers sound a fanfare at Carfax during Warship Week in February 1942 when Oxford exceeded its target of £1,250,000 by almost a quarter of a million pounds.

Saving paper was an early priority and the *Bicester Advertiser* was only available to order from 15 March 1940; in April the *Chipping Norton Advertiser* shrank in size because the publishers had been rationed to 30 per cent of the previous year's newsprint.[33] In Faringdon the Red Cross was setting up a central depot for waste paper in Swan Lane by the end of October 1939, and Thame Urban District Council voted to collect and bale waste paper separately in January 1940.[34] In urban areas dustmen usually collected paper as part of their regular rounds although their work was supplemented in Oxford by the Women's Voluntary Service which divided the city into twelve districts and organized house-to-house collections.[35] In Abingdon and elsewhere scouts and guides also became involved in the collection of waste paper.[36] Rural areas were heavily dependent on voluntary effort and in the Bartons, for example, the Barton and Worton scouts sold 35 tons of waste paper by the end of 1944, raising £120 in the process.[37] In Burford the Women's Institute organized the collection of paper and other materials for salvage.[38] Sometimes individuals took the lead; at Hook Norton in March 1940 Miss Baker and eight other ladies drove round the village in a farm cart and collected three loads, making £1 17s for the Navy League.[39]

Later in the war, other initiatives were taken to stimulate fresh public interest and increase the flow of waste paper for recycling. The Waste Paper Recovery Association held special competitions among local authorities which were consciously designed to involve householders and schoolchildren. In 1942, for example, Banbury came second in a three county contest and won a prize of £250

The war savings kiosk at the Northern Aluminium Company factory in Banbury during Wings for Victory Week in 1943. The workplace was a vital target for savings campaigns throughout the war.

by collecting more than 13½ lb of waste paper per head of population; in the same competition Henley collected 21 tons 10½ cwt of paper.[40] As the need became more desperate, book salvage became a priority and the Ministry of Supply held a special campaign in the county between 20 June and 4 July 1942. The campaign director, Mr Pike, remarked:

> In Oxfordshire, this great centre of learning, one expects a particularly heavy yield of old and unwanted books, many thousands of which are kept on shelves for sentimental or other reasons. I shall ask the public to give such books to the war effort and by so doing I anticipate at least a yield of not less than 150,000 books.[41]

His hopes were certainly fulfilled in Thame where over 70 tons of books were handed in during the fortnight and the pupils of John Hampden School won a prize for raising the most money.[42]

At the end of 1942 there was a rumour that national libraries would be requested to surrender works of fiction deposited under copyright. An official at the Bodleian expressed dismay:

> If any library is going to start throwing out works, the principle of a depository goes at once and the librarian would take a very great risk in throwing away something which would in the future be thought valuable.[43]

This contentious proposal was quietly shelved and the Bodleian Library was in fact a beneficiary from the huge Oxford Book Appeal held in March 1943,

Girls from the 5th East Oxford Girl Guides collecting waste paper for the Red Cross.

acquiring 497 books from the 417,405 that were collected. The book drive lasted a fortnight and was prefaced by a direct appeal:

MR WINSTON CHURCHILL HAS ASKED OXFORD TO
FIND
200,000
Books and Periodicals
During the fortnight of this appeal
the purpose being –
    1. To provide reading matter for our Armed Forces in England and abroad (including our boys who are Prisoners of War, and our Merchant Navy).
    2. To re-stock blitzed libraries.
    3. To ensure preservation of valuable books for posterity by careful scrutiny of every volume.
    4. To provide material for the munitions of war. . . . Look through your bookshelves and cupboards and tie up ALL the books that you can sacrifice, as well as the ones you can easily spare.[44]

Schoolchildren were involved as book stewards and eagerly carried bundles of books to school. The City Librarian, E.E. Skuce, praised their boundless enthusiasm, but his remarks suggest that this opinion was not universally shared:

I think one would be correct in saying that to the children of Oxford must go the credit of finding over a quarter of a million books. Now that the drive is over I hope that those of our citizens who found the children troublesome will forgive them and realise that the end justified the means.[45]

"Pulping—pulping—Forces—Bodleian—pulping—
Winskill's Circulating Library—pulping . . . "

*Book salvage benefits the Bodleian Library; a
cartoon in July 1943 illustrates one way of
sorting out the thousands of books that were
collected during special campaigns.*

The need to recycle metals into munitions became crucially important as the
country was cut off from its import markets. Lord Beaverbrook launched his
'Saucepans into Spitfires' campaign in July 1940, and within a matter of days Mrs
H. Goodhart of Chipping Norton had organized premises in Guildhall Place
where aluminium goods could be left.[46] Members of the WVS went round
Charlbury relieving householders of precious kitchen utensils, and in August
Thame sent over 3 cwt to the receiving depot in Oxford. The aluminium drive in
Oxford collected 4½ tons in a few weeks.[47]

Individuals and corporate bodies were also asked to donate scrap iron as a
patriotic duty and the Ministry of Supply appointed the local architect
W.A. Daft to organize the removal of railings in Oxford. He started with the
St John's College estate in North Oxford where he could deal most easily
with a single ground landlord; the City Council also proved obliging and in
July 1940 authorized the removal of railings from the Martyrs' Memorial,
the old churchyard at The Plain and the underground toilets at Rewley
Road.[48] The University also scrapped tons of iron railings from its buildings
and old iron bookcases from the basement of the Ashmolean Museum.[49] The
head teacher at Summertown School noted the removal of its railings for
munitions in June 1940, and by the autumn Oxford had generated 1,000 tons
of scrap iron.[50] A mania for collecting spread across the county like wildfire,
and at the July meeting of Henley Rural District Council Mrs H.G. Reade of
Ipsden

raised the question of collection of scrap from outlying farms. She added that
she was removing the iron railings from the tombs of some of her ancestors in
the churchyard.[51]

Workmen removing the railings from an Oxford street. The photograph was probably taken early in 1942 after the salvage of railings had been made compulsory.

Boys from Wantage Church School collected 4 tons of scrap iron by July 1940 and children at Littlemore managed to amass over 4 tons in two days; in Benson villagers were even prepared to sacrifice the 1887 Coronation lamp to the war effort.[52]

Many householders, however, did not consider their railings to be redundant and, with the slogan 'Don't Rail, Part with your Railings', the Mayor of Oxford launched a new appeal in the spring of 1941.[53] The response failed to match the country's urgent need for scrap metal and the compulsory removal of railings was introduced, contrary to the view expressed by Mrs Johnstone at a Banbury Rural District Council meeting in November 1941: 'People would rather give than have things snatched from them – it is not an English practice to snatch.'[54] In future railings were only to be kept if they contributed to public safety or were of sufficient architectural or historic interest. At Charlbury Victorian railings round the Playing Close were therefore preserved as a protection for local children and railings at The Crescent in Park Town, Oxford, survived because passers-by might otherwise have fallen into semi-basements in the black-out.[55] A panel of architects secured the retention of historic ironwork at the Bodleian Library and the Sheldonian Theatre, and in Eynsham Oxford Diocese stepped in to prevent the removal of the railings in front of the church and war memorial.[56] At Thame, on the other hand, the war memorial railings were taken down in spite of angry public protest and railings were removed at the bottom of Whitchurch School playground in January 1943, leaving it open to the public path.[57]

Waste not, want not; separation of the household refuse by Oxford dustmen on their rounds.

Every opportunity was taken to collect and recycle other salvageable materials. At Henley in 1940 a local farmer was collecting the town's kitchen waste for pig swill and employees of Oxford City's Cleansing Department fed pigs with the vegetable refuse that they collected from householders.[58] People were encouraged from the first to separate their rubbish into categories such as paper and rags, bones, metal and food waste in order to make it easier to sort and salvage. From May 1942 it became a punishable offence under the Waste Paper Order to put paper into refuse bins and offenders were liable to fines ranging from £100 to £500 or imprisonment for between three months and two years.[59] Drinkers were urged to put the stoppers back in returnable bottles in order to save rubber, and in January 1942 efforts were being made to salvage milk bottle tops for munitions; the *Oxford Mail* asked householders to clean and return metal tops to the milkman and to put cardboard ones out with the waste paper.[60] A special appeal was made for brass, copper, bronze and lead in October 1942.[61] The Ministry of Supply's most unlikely appeal, however, was probably its request for old binoculars for the forces in January 1941; Regional Binocular Officer R.H. Bailey reported that 3,000 pairs had been donated in the Southern Area, but more glasses are wanted to meet the growing needs of the Forces, and more people must help us to meet these needs. I ask every owner of a pair of glasses not now being used to help the nation to bring them out to-day.[62]

As part of Salute the Soldier Week in June 1944 Henley sent greetings cards to servicemen and women who came from the town and the surrounding district. Private Victor Rathbone, a Henley man who was serving in Italy with the Royal Engineers, was sufficiently touched by the gesture to return his thanks and commented that,

if the people of Henley will continue to do their share of saving, we can assure them the fighting boys of Henley-on-Thames will do their share to get this lot finished with so that we may return to our good old home town.[63]

Regardless of their economic importance, the wartime programmes of savings and salvage therefore served to unite the civilian population with the military in a common struggle for victory. At the end of the war, however, the vast salvaging machine had suddenly to be thrown into reverse, and by November 1945 Cowley's Metal and Produce Recovery Depot was beginning to turn 'Spitfires into Saucepans'.[64]

CHAPTER EIGHT

Everyday Life

The spirit of 'Make Do and Mend' permeated virtually all aspects of everyday life as the nation struggled with an insufficiency of commodities which had been taken for granted in peacetime. Food, clothing and furniture were rationed, the use of private cars was heavily restricted, public transport services were reduced and recreational opportunities were limited. In many ways, life became dreary and seemingly dominated by endless queues, but there was, at the same time, a real sense of common purpose and always an urge to 'Keep Smiling Through'.

At the end of August 1939 the *Oxford Mail* noted a rush to the shops to buy food in case of war[1] and rationing was inevitable if scarce resources were to be equally shared. A network of regional and local Food Control Committees was established by the Ministry of Food to organize the distribution of food, and railside cold stores were later built at Kennington and South Leigh. The first ration books in Oxford were issued in October 1939.[2] In November the *Witney Gazette* explained to readers that there were three types of ration book, one for adults and older children, another for children under six and a third for people such as lorry drivers, commercial travellers and variety artists who were not always living at home.[3] Householders were ordered to register with a particular grocer for the supply of bacon, ham, butter and sugar by 23 November and rationing was introduced on 8 January 1940.[4] Everything seemed to go quite smoothly in Oxfordshire and many people welcomed 'Coupon Monday' as an end to favouritism.[5] Initially, each person was allowed a weekly ration of 4 oz of ham or bacon, 4 oz of butter and 12 oz of sugar and there were inevitably complaints that this was not enough. The *Faringdon Advertiser* countered the grumblers by arguing that rationing was at least scrupulously fair and that 'it is up to everyone to "make the best of it"'.[6]

As the war progressed more foods had to be rationed and allowances fluctuated according to the availability of each commodity. Meat rationing was introduced in March 1940 and limited each individual to 1s 10d worth per week. Tea (2 oz) and cooking fat or margarine (2 oz) were put on the ration in July 1940. Preserves such as jam, marmalade and syrup were rationed from March 1941 and cheese, limited at first to a miserly 1 oz per person per week, joined the list in May.[7] E.J. Lainchbury recalled that a typical week's ration for one person in 1941 was '½ lb sugar, 2 oz tea, ¼ lb fat including not more than 2 oz butter or margarine, 6 oz bacon, ¼ lb jam, ¼ lb cheese, 3½ pints milk'.[8]

These basic foods had to be obtained from the registered suppliers specified in the ration book, but the points system introduced in December 1941 gave the customer an element of choice when buying commodities such as tinned meat,

The sugar store at Frank Cooper's Victoria Works in Oxford in September 1942. With sugar on the ration from January 1940, a scene like this would have been beyond the wildest dreams of anyone with a sweet tooth.

fish, vegetables and biscuits. Each person was given sixteen, later twenty, points a month which could be 'spent' at any shop and products were given a points value; 1 lb of dried fruit was, for example, worth 8 points, 1 lb of biscuits 8 points and 1 lb of tinned meat 12 points.[9]

The importance of ensuring a fair distribution of food was stressed in the regular Situation Reports which Oxford's Chief Constable sent to the Home Office. In December 1940 he warned that there was considerable resentment about the shortage of cheese, biscuits, chocolate and sweets. On 2 March 1941 he returned to the same theme, contrasting the adequate food supplies in hotels and restaurants with the queues outside:

> With eggs, too, whilst retailers are eking out two or three a week to their customers, restaurants are apparently getting enough to provide for cocktail mixing. . . . In addition, the price of fish is prohibitive to the poor and I seriously suggest that this distinction between the rich and the poor in the supply and distribution of food will, if not soon attended to, lead to trouble.

Such warnings underlined the need for food control, and since the rationing of preserves was introduced in March Whitehall must have received the County Controller's report at the end of that month with some satisfaction:

Food rationing appears to be fairly satisfactory, there is already some comment on the fact that jam, marmalade and syrup can now be obtained since being included on the list of rationed goods, whereas previously it was practically unobtainable.[10]

An enormous bureaucracy was of course needed to oversee rationing and shopkeepers were committed to a tiresome and time-consuming amount of paperwork. An official price was set for virtually every commodity and in 1942, for instance, Fruit Preservation Centres organized by the Oxfordshire Federation of Women's Institutes had to be warned:

Wild blackberries: The official maximum price for these has now been fixed at 3½d per lb. This price is for both growers and pickers.[11]

To exceed the official price was to invite prosecution and a typical case occurred in Oxford Cattle Market in September 1940. Mrs Vera Chambers, a clerk employed by the Oxford Food Control Committee, bought half a dozen eggs for 1s 9d and each egg was subsequently found to weigh less than 2 oz. Both the stallholder and his wife were fined a total of £3 for this offence.[12]

In June 1940 a Banbury café proprietor was fined £100 on ten counts of using more sugar in a week than was permitted under the Rationing Order of 1939.[13] Black market trading was deterred by making it an offence to sell rationed goods without the appropriate coupons being cancelled. Both the butcher Eric Stanley and his customer, Mrs Goodchild of Swerford, were therefore fined in February 1943 after he delivered meat while she was out and then forgot to ask for her ration book on subsequent visits.[14] A special application had to be made for any variation to the basic ration, and on 8 October 1940 A.J. Basford of the Witney Rural Food Committee sent this permit to Messrs Hambidge & Son, High Street, Burford:

You are authorised to supply

to E. Moore
10 The Lease
Burford

the following rationed goods for a Wedding Reception to be held at 10 The Lease, Burford, on October 19th, 1940.

2 oz Butter
¼ lb Tea
½ lb Sugar.[15]

The local committees were, to some extent, a law unto themselves and in April 1940 the Banbury Rural Food Committee had to give no explanation when it refused to supply a traveller's ration book to a temporary parlourmaid who was moving regularly from place to place.[16]

However equitable the distribution of food, shortages became unavoidable and queues ubiquitous. On 7 February 1941 H.W.B. Joseph, Fellow of New College, complained that he had only been able to buy ¼ lb of cheese instead of the usual 1 lb and reported paying 7d a pound for poor quality Bramley seedlings.[17]

Oxfordshire housewives were warned in November 1940 of a sudden drastic cut in milk supplies, and in April 1943 milkless days, together with ½ pint bottles, were introduced in Oxford.[18] From June 1941 customers were expected to bring their own sugar into cafés[19] and in Burford, for example, matches, cigarettes, candles, salt, pepper, vinegar, cornflour and toilet paper were difficult to come by:

> This last gave rise to an amusing incident, when a lady in an expensive fur coat was seen leaving a friend's house clutching a rare roll to her bosom.[20]

Supplies of fresh fish in Thame were so inadequate in 1942 that the Urban District Council made representations to the Ministry of Food, only to be told that the situation was universal.[21] The unsatisfactory meat supply in Bicester aroused the wrath of the local Chamber of Commerce in February 1940 and John Taylor remarked that the frozen lamb was 'Graf Spee stock' because it should, like the German pocket battleship, have been scuttled;[22] in Oxford the butcher S.J. Haynes of No. 25 Little Clarendon Street published a cartoon advertisement begging customers DON'T SHOOT YOUR BUTCHER![23] The egg became such a rarity that it inspired this 'Ode to an Egg' in March 1942:

> Oh, precious Egg! Delectable,
> With flavour unforgettable!
> That creamy white, that golden yolk,
> Food too rich for common folk.
> Kings and princes all aver
> Eggs to caviare they prefer.

Don't shoot your butcher! An advertisement in self-defence by an Oxford tradesman who was unable to provide the service that he and his customers wanted because of meat shortages.

With what solemn awe at last
We eat our monthly Egg for breakfast –
Poached or scrambled, sometimes fried,
Or as an omelette disguised;
Or, with equal ceremony
Have it boiled for our tea.

They tell me that in days of yore
Eggs could be purchased by the score.
Your public speaker lived in dread
Of having eggs thrown at his head.
Gone are those days; now we treasure
You, source of gastronomic pleasure.

Oh, shapely Egg! It seems a sin
To break your shell so white and thin;
But as, alas, you would not keep
Your flavour long, I bury scruples deep;
Enjoy your riches while I may,
And hope for more another day.[24]

While eggs grew scarce, the importing of foreign fruit virtually ceased and when Leading Stoker Philip Martin came home on leave with a bunch of bananas, he was able to sell it and raise funds for the Red Cross.[25] Oranges were so prized that even the possible arrival of a consignment was eagerly reported in the *Oxford Mail* in October 1941 and the Queen was given a single orange as a present when she visited the Churchill Hospital in July 1944.[26] Some products became unobtainable, and in October 1942 Frank Cooper Ltd was forced to announce:

'OXFORD' MARMALADE

Owing to the requisitioning of our
factory at Oxford by the Government
we regret that the manufacture of
'Oxford' Marmalade must cease until
after the War.[27]

The shortage of many foods made shopping a lengthy and challenging experience. S.P.B. Mais recalled that, in Oxford,

We stood in endless queues in the cold, draughty market waiting for fish which was sold out before we reached the slab, the shops with whom we were registered making it clear that it was only because of their courtesy and kindness that we were able to procure any food at all.[28]

At the butchers, Phyl Surman would count the number of people in front of her and then note how many portions of offal were displayed on the trays; in this way she could assess whether it was to be her lucky day.[29] Waits of forty-five minutes were a regular feature of the Oxford shopper's life in 1943, and because 'queue-forming was becoming a habit and a disease' there was even an unsuccessful attempt in July 1941 to ban all queueing except for buses in central Oxford. Councillor King remarked that invasion by queues was unpleasant for the shopkeeper, blocked access to neighbouring shops and was, for the most part, inessential.[30] Tempers frayed easily in these circumstances and there were frequent allegations of 'under the counter' or 'hush-hush' sales. One furious Oxford housewife rushed to a shop where cherries were reported to be on sale only to be told that they had sold out; after she had bought a few other things she was asked quietly whether she would like some cherries and, overcoming her disgust at this chicanery, she bought a pound 'for the children's sake'.[31] Acting on rumour was one strategy for survival, another was the technique adopted in Oxford by Josep Trueta's wife:

> I remember that whenever Amelia went to the butcher, she used to put on what we called her 'butcher's eyes' – that is, she would try to look hungry and miserable in the hope that he would add a few ounces more to the ration.[32]

Shopping was still more difficult for war workers who had little or no time to queue and there were lengthy discussions on this issue in Banbury between Union representatives at the Northern Aluminium Company and traders in the town. In February 1942 local grocers recommended that shoppers register with just one trader instead of trying to secure more unrationed goods by registering with different firms for different products. War workers were also advised to place orders a day or two in advance and were promised a fair share of unrationed goods.[33]

People with allotments or sizeable gardens could improve their diet by growing some of their own food, and there was an increase in animal-keeping. In Burford the old tradition of keeping hens and pigs in backyards made a come-back, defying early doubts as to whether the food control bureaucracy would permit someone with a pig to kill it and keep the meat for home consumption.[34] At J.R.R. Tolkien's house in North Oxford 'hens were installed in the garden to increase the supply of eggs', and the Truetas in Headington also kept hens, on one occasion using an umbrella to drive a fox away from their hen-house.[35]

A battery of national and local campaigns set out to improve the nation's health by giving advice about nutrition and urging housewives to make the most of the foods that were still available. The Ministry of Food, headed by the energetic Lord Woolton, drove home the message that 'Food is a Munition of War':

> Just as surely as a soldier, a sailor or an airman, you and your family can help to win the war. How? . . . With what? With your war munition – food. When you see that it is used rightly in keeping your family and yourself healthy and satisfied, and that not a bit is wasted, you can feel proud of doing an important job towards bringing victory nearer.

The Ministry organized cookery demonstrations throughout the country, issued a series of recipe leaflets, and in 1943 published *Wise Eating in Wartime*, a booklet containing fifteen of the 'Kitchen Front' broadcasts by Dr Charles Hill, 'The Radio Doctor'. These cheerful talks, which went out every weekday morning at 8.15, had such titles as 'Offal Good Value for Money', 'What can we do with Milk?', 'Cheese – can you Beat it?' and 'Green Leaves make Rosy Cheeks'. Dr Hill stressed the need for variety, arguing that 'Repetition day after day of the same foods, cooked and dished in the same way, is enough to drive a man to drink – and it sometimes does'. Housewives were deluged with 'Food Facts' in local newspapers and commercial recipe books such as *Win-the-War Cookery*, while characters like Dr Carrot and Potato Pete urged a greater use of the vegetables that were readily available. Potato Pete was particularly ingenious and suggested recipes for every meal of the day, including such delicacies as Potato Toppings for Toast, Pink and Green Puree, Potato and Spinach Croquettes, Potato Sandwich Spread, Hot Potato Salad, Potato Soup and Surprise Potato Balls.[36]

The battle for healthy eating was reinforced by local initiatives, and in 1940 Oxfordshire Education Committee arranged a series of wartime cookery demonstrations all over the county which provided information about making sugarless puddings, cooking with a hay box and preserving fruit and vegetables.[37] In Oxford practical demonstrations at the School of Technology in St Ebbe's aimed to show people how to make the most of rationed foods and to keep the family fighting fit in days of shortages.[38] Women's groups provided a local focus for the campaign and in February 1940, for instance, members of Banbury

Apple Week display in the window of the County Horticultural Department in New Road, Oxford, in November 1944.

Townswomen's Guild met to discuss cookery in wartime, hearing a talk from Miss Wiseman and bringing recipes of their own.[39]

None of this endeavour could entirely disguise the increased monotony of the average diet. As fresh produce became scarce, the consumer had increasingly to accept such things as butter substitute, dried eggs and Household, or National Dried, Milk. Spam, or SPiced hAM, was first imported from the United States as a tinned replacement for fresh meat in 1942.[40] At Ewelme early in 1943 there was a general feeling that 'Food was getting less interesting, and we were making jokes about Spam and Dried Eggs'.[41] Even the author of Ministry of Food approved recipes in *Cookery Service Notes No. 38* was forced to admit that dried eggs and milk would not give the same results as their natural equivalents and introduced a sponge recipe with the warning:

> I must make it clear that with wartime rations you cannot make a real sponge mixture unless you save up the necessary ingredients, including shell eggs, and then follow a good pre-war recipe. The recipe which follows is definitely a wartime substitute, but when spread with jam will help to make a nice change at tea-time.[42]

Anyone with a sweet tooth became accustomed to sugarless recipes and Phyl Surman's wedding cake had to be 'iced' with a chocolate covering; to soften the blow, however,

> the cake was covered by a white cardboard edifice resembling sugared icing and this was lifted off by the eaters when the cake was cut.[43]

The fact that the nation's diet was boring was ultimately less important than whether it was adequate. In 1940 Dr Hugh Sinclair, who ran the Oxford Nutritional Survey from the University's Department of Biochemistry, suggested that a biscuit containing all the essential vitamins should be developed and issued to the public. Nothing came of that proposal, but Sinclair's survey helped to inform national food policy during the war, thus contributing to what Sir Donald Acheson has described as 'the most notably beneficial intervention of government in nutrition so far recorded anywhere'.[44] Instead of receiving special biscuits, much of the population was given access to Government-aided communal feeding centres which were generally called British Restaurants, although in Oxford they were known as Municipal Restaurants. These establishments were intended to minimize the waste of food and they were especially useful to householders who no longer had to agonize over the problem of providing an adequate evening meal for billeted war workers and evacuees; they also reduced friction over cooking arrangements in shared houses and provided somewhere else for billetees to go at weekends when relatives visited.[45] Oxford's first restaurant of this kind opened in the Cowley Road Congregational Schoolroom in January 1941 and offered a two-course lunch for 9d, or just 4d for children.[46] Other Municipal Restaurants were opened in Oxford, initially in converted premises such as the Rose Hill Community Centre, the New Road Baptist Church and the Majestic Cinema, but purpose-built prefabricated concrete structures were later provided, for example, at York Place and at the Canal Wharf in New Road. In March 1944 it was

The newly built Municipal Restaurant on the Canal Wharf in New Road, Oxford, in November 1943.

announced that the city's restaurants had served 799,000 meals in the last eight months, making a profit of 1¼*d* per meal.[47]

The British Restaurant became a feature of many Oxfordshire communities including Henley, Burford, Chinnor, Charlbury and Shipton-under-Wychwood. Woodstock's British Restaurant opened on 8 December 1940 with the active support of the Duchess of Marlborough and her daughter, Lady Sarah; the duke also helped by providing the vegetables and the services of an electrician.[48] At Banbury a new British Restaurant was opened by the mayor in January 1943:

> The menu, which we are given to understand was a typical example of that to be obtained daily, consisted of roast beef or mutton, baked and boiled potatoes, and brussel sprouts. The dessert course was a choice of milk pudding or baked jam roll and custard. It was followed by tea or coffee, and the price for this meal, which was appetisingly served and much enjoyed, will be normally 1*s* 3*d*.
>
> The buildings throughout are decorated in bright sunshine yellow, with woodwork in green. At either end of the dining hall and in the vestibule appropriate artistic paintings have been designed and executed by Miss D.J. Milne, ARCA, headmistress of the Technical Institute.[49]

In order to cover the more scattered population beyond the reach of the British Restaurants, Oxfordshire pioneered the Meat Pie Scheme for agricultural workers which was later adopted by Lord Woolton as the basis for a national plan. Encouraged by the personal interest of Lord Macclesfield, the Chairman of

Oxfordshire County Council, the scheme was launched in January 1941 in five villages near Chipping Norton. Mr Webb, the baker in Chadlington, and Mr Hackling, the Churchill baker, baked pies for their villages and the other places where they delivered, and Women's Voluntary Service representatives sold them twice weekly at stated times and places. Customers were allowed four pies a week and these were duly added to the men's lunches. The scheme was a tremendous success and in the first five months no fewer than 549 dozen pies were sold, making a profit of £38 6s 7d for the County Council. The number of Oxfordshire villages served rose to 65 by the end of May 1941, and to 175 in October 1942 when 16,000 meat pies a week were being consumed.[50] It was noted in Burford, however, that farmworkers' initial enthusiasm for the pies 'gradually fell off, probably due to lack of variety'.[51]

Berkshire County Council established large Feeding Depots, one of them being located in the Market Square at Wantage. The Wantage depot had a staff of sixteen in October 1942 and was preparing 2,100 two-course meals and a further 440 meat pies a day; these were then delivered to surrounding villages by a fleet of Chevrolet vans. Oxfordshire planned similar facilities but was forced to change its policy, causing an exasperated Clerk to the County Council to criticize 'the rather vague and sometimes conflicting instructions which they have received from the Ministry of Food'.[52] Instead, the network of British Restaurants provided cooking centres for nearby villages, and at Wootton, for example,

> The sending out of school dinners by a travelling canteen from the British Restaurant at Woodstock simplified things a great deal for women working on the land, who had children to arrange for.[53]

Subsidized school dinners were described by Lord Woolton as being 'a definite part of major policy which is based on the nutritional requirements of the rising generation', and by June 1942 seventy Oxfordshire schools had canteens and 4,200 children were receiving dinner every day.[54] In 1944 many School Medical Officers noted the results with approval:

> During the last few years my impression is that the health of the school children has improved rather than deteriorated. . . . I think I have noticed a considerable improvement where school dinners have been provided and taken by most children.
> I have noticed the difference in the poorer families since the innovation of school dinners. I think it is an excellent thing in the country, as many children have to come quite a long way to school.
> There was a very marked improvement in children's nutrition where dinners (cooked at school) were available. . . . I do feel that school dinners (cooked at school) have done a great deal for the children during the war years.[55]

Plans for emergency feeding formed one aspect of wartime food policy that was never tested. Each local authority's scheme was based on the assumption that up to 10 per cent of the population might need to be fed if air raids demolished key buildings or crippled gas and electricity supplies. In Oxfordshire there were plans to cater for up to 16,400 people by using British Restaurants as cooking centres and rushing insulated containers from dispersed stores at Shirburn Castle and Gosford Hill School. Alternative centres were identified in case the British Restaurants were destroyed and at Chipping Norton, for instance, Reg's Café, with a normal cooking capacity for 100 people, would have an emergency capacity of 800; the capacity of the Cotswold Café at Enstone would be increased similarly from 20 people to between 200 and 400. At Henley there were plans to operate a twenty-four-hour service at the British Restaurant which could prepare 1,000 meals every three hours for distribution in the county's containers; at the same time, a soup kitchen in the Town Hall would provide 60 gallons of soup or stew every three hours and the Town Clerk advised that 'fried fish shops in the Borough would cooperate in the cooking and quick service of plain food'. Banbury, with its own target of 1,850 people to feed, established five dispersed feeding centres and two reserve premises and stored a semi-mobile canteen at Bloxham's Yard, Warwick Road, which could have produced meals for 500 if the need had arisen.[56]

Each village had its own emergency feeding arrangements and the Kirtlington Invasion Committee's War Book issued in 1942 listed Mrs Budgett as Food Executive Officer and Mrs Douglas as Deputy. The village hall and Kirtlington Park were the identified emergency feeding centres and the store of local reserves were in Kirtlington Park, 'known to Messrs Deering, Scarrott and Dow'; in addition, there were said to be 'good reserves of potatoes, vegetables, and meat (on the hoof)'.[57] At Ewelme the emergency food supply was in the chapel next to

A woman uses coupons to buy shoes at an Oxford shop in June 1941 when the purchase of new clothing was first rationed.

Bennett's stores and at least one person thought longingly of the sugar that was so near and yet so far.[58]

The restrictions and monotony of the wartime diet were eventually paralleled by the limited availability of new clothing and furniture. In the early stages of the war, buying clothes provided one means of escapism and as food rationing was introduced in early 1940, Kinch's the tailors in Bicester advertised their wares in a little poem:

> While some foods are hard to get
> Our wants give way to rations
> Your needs in Tailored Clothes are met
> With Kinch's Rational Fashions.[59]

As factories and labour were increasingly diverted into war work, however, fashion items became scarce and more expensive. In October 1939, for example, F. Cape & Co., the Oxford drapers, notified their branches about the increased prices of particular brands of ladies' hosiery:

	old price	new
Marian	11¾	1/4¾
Evelyn	1/11½	2/9
Bondor	3/3	3/11
Diana	2/11½	3/11
Allnumbers	3/11½	4/11[60]

A year later there was chaos in Oxford after the announcement that from 1 December no further supplies of pure silk stockings would be available:

> At some shops there were crowds four deep, and the scene was reminiscent of the summer sales and the Christmas rush. . . . At Elliston and Cavell's the assault was so great that the assistants had to call for a cessation of hostilities, and the counter was closed down for two hours so that the girls might recuperate.
>
> 'I have never known anything like it,' a shopwalker told me. 'Some women were even prepared to pay nearly 10s a pair. Thousands of pairs must have been sold in Oxford on Saturday.'[61]

Savings campaigns tried to persuade the nation that it was unpatriotic to squander money on unnecessary items and from 1 June 1941 new clothes were only available 'on coupons'. Under this system, each person received a yearly allocation of sixty-six coupons which was intended to provide one complete new outfit a year.[62] In March 1942, however, the ration was cut to just fifty-one coupons and orders were made to ban double-breasted suits and turn-ups and to reduce the number of pockets in new garments; the Government argued that this action would release 50,000 workers from the textile industry and enable merchant ships to concentrate on importing more urgently needed war supplies.[63] Each item of clothing was given a points value according to the amount of labour and material needed in its production; thus, a man's overcoat required 16 coupons, a pair of trousers 8, a skirt 7 and a pair of underpants 4.[64]

In 1942 a range of 'Utility' clothing was introduced using standard patterns to save cloth, buttons and other materials, but it became particularly difficult to buy new shoes. In April 1943 the Oxford & District Co-operative Society announced the launch of a children's shoe exchange scheme in Headington, advising intending patrons that 'In the Interests of General Health all footwear will be disinfected upon receipt'.[65] Milwards in Bell Street, Henley, advised women customers in January 1944:

They're flying to victory in your bootees! That's why there are no fleece-lined bootees. We offer you a substitute, for the coming colder weather, in wood-soled shoes. They are warm, comfortable, sturdy and very stylish.[66]

The black market was one way round these shortages and there existed a lively, illegal trade in clothing coupons; for the most part, though, the slogan 'Make Do and Mend' became the standard reply to anyone wanting new clothes. Oxfordshire County Council appointed Mrs Badger to travel to women's groups like Burford WI and give advice about conserving, altering and patching clothes.[67] In 1943 the Board of Trade published a booklet entitled *Make Do and Mend*, which contained dozens of useful hints about such things as turning men's clothes into women's, curing bagginess in skirts or giving new life to an old coat. The suggestions given in the section 'Cutting-Down for the Children' showed particular ingenuity:

Bathing wraps can be made into children's dressing gowns.
Grey flannel trousers will make children's knickers and skirts.
Mackintoshes will cut down for a child's waterproof coat or cape with pixie hood to match.
Plus-fours would make two pairs of shorts for a schoolboy.
Pyjama legs will make children's vests.
An old skirt will make one pair of knickers and a little play-skirt for a seven-year-old.
Vest and combination tops will make bodices on to which a little girl's or a small boy's knickers will button.
Washing-silk dresses make up into gay pyjamas for children.[68]

Newspaper advertisements and patterns encouraged women to alter coats, make pinafore frocks which could 'disguise a multitude of short-comings', prolong the life of their corsets and create economy undies. This last example of clothes economy offered a pattern for making a bra and panty set out of an old evening frock:

You will save your coupons, and will probably manage two sets from it, especially if it has one of those very full skirts which were so fashionable in pre-war days.[69]

For those women whose silk stockings were beyond repair, there was the option noted in Burford of wearing cheaper ones inside out since this made them look less shiny and more exclusive. Other women simply painted their legs with coffee or suntan lotion and asked a good friend with a steady hand to apply the 'seam' with an eyebrow pencil.[70]

Shortages of material led to the rationing of towels and tea towels in June 1942 and within a year women were being asked to bring their own towels to H.L. Chaplin's hairdressing salon in Woodstock Road, Oxford. Strange's in Market Street, too, were on the verge of adopting a 'No towel, No shampoo' rule because of the scarcity of towels.[71] As a further refinement of rationing, laundry zoning was tested in Oxford from May 1943, obliging customers to deal only with the firm to which they were allocated. The scheme attracted immense criticism and in November a petition from 327 East Oxford residents to the city's MP, Quintin Hogg, alleged that it had led to the 'loss and ruination of articles'. Despite the complaints, laundry zoning remained in force in Oxford but the experiment was not repeated elsewhere.[72]

Furniture-making was not seen as a wartime priority and timber imports ceased in July 1940. The Board of Trade permitted the manufacture of only twenty-two essential items from 1942, and strict price controls were enforced. 'Utility Furniture' was introduced to provide durable furniture at a reasonable price, but at least one purchaser of a sideboard noticed that when 'the sun shone on the back under the thin oak veneer, I could distinctly see the lettering "Apples"'.[73] Other household necessities like mattresses, sheets, blankets, curtain material and floor covering became almost impossible to obtain without 'Priority Dockets' which were issued only to the bombed-out or to those who were setting up home for the first time. In Kidlington Phyl Surman as a wartime bride remembered being given enough dockets to buy three sheets, two blankets and sufficient lino and curtaining for two rooms.[74]

Privation extended into the home through constant reminders to save fuel and water. There was just one week's supply of coal in Charlbury in March 1941, and in Shipton-under-Wychwood 650 consumers were sharing a mere 16 tons; in the Bartons area only three tons of coal were left for 400 households.[75] This crisis was due mainly to transport congestion but, from the middle of 1941, an attempt was made to limit demand by prescribing maximum monthly deliveries of household coal to each consumer. Fuel economy was another way of reducing consumption and a special display was held in Banbury Town Hall in November 1942:

> A realistic bedroom scene enjoins abstemption from the not uncommon habit of reading in bed. . . . A drawing-room scene illustrates the economy effect of neighbourly co-operation; a kitchen in another bay shows that 40 per cent fuel saving can be effected by 'lagging' hot water storage tanks.[76]

The Government were reluctant to ration the domestic consumption of gas and electricity for political and administrative reasons, and relied instead on voluntary economy by the consumer. In November 1944 the Wessex Electricity Co. published a cartoon advertisement in the *Oxford Mail* showing an Eskimo family seeing off a pipe-smoking commuter on snow shoes; the caption warned, 'We know it's cold but don't use your electric fire between 8 a.m. and 1 p.m.'[77] In the same way, water was seen as a resource to be conserved and in July 1940 the City Engineer warned Oxford people to use less or he would be forced to reduce supplies. It was considered unpatriotic to luxuriate in a deep bath and the diary of

Fuel Economy exhibition in Oxford Town Hall in November 1942. Graphic displays urge visitors to save coal and water, and warn that an unlagged tank will help Hitler.

one housewife's hectic day ended with the entry: '10.45 p.m. Find it difficult to sing in five inches of bath water'.[78]

Outside the home the dislocation of normal transport was an everyday reminder of wartime conditions. Bus and rail services were curtailed from the first and, for this reason, the enterprising Bowne's Hairdressing Saloon in Bicester was offering to convey customers to and from their appointments in October 1939.[79] Shortage of vehicles and staff made the Oxford bus service a regular subject of complaint and there were further objections in August 1941 when it was announced that the last buses would leave at 9.30 p.m. in order to conserve petrol. Stanley Dorrill protested on behalf of the New Theatre and J. Cooklin, manager of the Super Cinema, argued that the last house would be lost:

> People come to this cinema from as far afield as Banbury, Woodstock and Abingdon, and many of them cannot come in until the evening. . . . The bus service is bad enough as it is. . . . I, myself, often have to walk home at night.[80]

'Save It' display in the foyer of the Sterling Cinema at Kidlington in January 1943. On the left, a panel illustrates HMS Enterprise, *the warship adopted by the City of Oxford.*

The groundswell of complaint developed into a petition to the Mayor of Oxford from 450 people, drawing attention to 'the chaotic condition of the bus service' and 'the continual queues' and stating that 'deep resentment is now felt by every class of resident'. The bus company's response stressed that under-staffing was the major problem and a special effort was being made to recruit women as conductors and drivers; the situation had been made worse, however, by a 25 per cent increase in passenger numbers and the nuisance caused by 'short-distance riders'. The Regional Transport Commissioner drew much of the sting from the protest by stating that bus services in Oxford compared favourably with those in Reading and Aylesbury and he remarked that 'the luxuries of total peace cannot be expected during total war'. In February 1942 the city's Watch Committee was therefore forced to conclude that the company should continue to make every effort to provide efficient services, but 'there was little likelihood of any permanent improvement being effected'.[81]

The company's hands were also tied by strict fuel rationing and for this reason the Regional Transport Commissioner would only allow a supplementary bus service between Carfax and Ferry Hinksey Road at peak hours when Butlin's Amusement Park was at Botley Road Recreation Ground in July 1943.[82]

Reduced services inevitably meant overcrowding on the remaining buses, and to prevent arguments on the pavement a special by-law made queueing for buses compulsory in Oxford from May 1941:

> When six or more persons are waiting in any street in the City of Oxford to enter a public vehicle at any stopping place, stand, or terminus, they shall form and keep a queue or line of not more than two abreast on the footway of such street. . . .
>
> A person shall not take or endeavour to take any position in a queue or line otherwise than behind the persons already forming the same, or enter any public vehicle before any other person desiring to enter the same vehicle who stood in front of him in such queue or line.
>
> Every person who shall offend against any of these by-laws shall be liable on summary conviction to a fine not exceeding forty shillings.[83]

One woman returning to Enstone from a shopping expedition in Oxford recalled that 'the bus became so full that people had to sit on the stairs'.[84] In 1943 Kiddington people were complaining that the Oxford bus was always full by the time it reached them and that they could not visit friends in hospital, attend hospital appointments or get their food rations.[85] The black-out added to the difficulties of potential passengers since the reduced lighting of destination boxes was intended to make the wording 'just readable at 100 feet'; bus drivers had similar problems in identifying waiting passengers, and in September 1939 the *Witney Gazette* was advising people to wave white handkerchiefs which were visible for 30 to 40 yd.[86]

Conditions on Oxford's buses reached a low point in February 1943 with the introduction on some routes of gas-producer buses that conserved petrol. With their coal-gas trailers, known familiarly as chestnut roasters, these slow and stop buses attracted many complaints like this one from the *Oxford Mail*'s Diarist in January 1944:

> About 5.40 p.m. the queue, the very long queue, waiting outside the Post Office in St Aldate's was rewarded by the sight of a gas-producer bus crawling painfully up St Aldate's. The queue piled into the bus, the conductress rang the bell and we set off, travelled about a yard, and then stopped. There followed what in modern military parlance is termed 'inching' – progress literally a few inches at a time. Within eight minutes the bus had crawled as far as Carfax, halted, as the red light was on, and when the green appeared remained immovable.

After a lengthy campaign which focused on the increased use of rubber, the waste of passengers' time and the irritation caused, there were great rejoicings in September 1944 when the gas-producer buses were finally consigned to oblivion.[87]

Passenger train services were generally reduced to enable the railways to carry a huge increase in freight and military traffic. On the Henley branch, for example,

One of the gas-producer buses which were introduced in Oxford to save fuel in 1943. They were very unreliable and were universally loathed.

three out of four through trains to Paddington were immediately cut from the timetable, and fewer trains continued beyond Witney to Fairford.[88] Normal services were also liable to disruption as the American J.F. Fulton discovered to his cost in 1940:

> Wednesday, October 23rd. I have tried to be optimistic about trains here during the War and this morning made the mistake of attempting to reach Reading on a local. The 8.40, as I discovered at the last minute, does not stop there. This was nearly an hour late in leaving, and the 8.50 departed at 9.45. . . . On reaching Didcot I became even more frantic on learning that the connecting train was also an hour late and was not expected until 11.

At this stage Fulton abandoned the railway and happily secured a lift from 'an extraordinarily attractive woman . . . in the blue uniform of the WVS'. Punctuality standards were so poor that when Fulton's train from Oxford to Cambridge was thirty minutes late, he considered it to be 'the first train I had been on in England that arrived more or less on time'.[89]

Although there were fewer trains, passenger numbers continued to rise because the wartime railways performed such a vital role linking service personnel, war workers and evacuees with their families. Trains became so crowded by the autumn of 1941 that it seemed necessary to try to deter intending travellers.

Rationing was felt to be impracticable and the Government opted instead to ask people 'Is Your Journey Really Necessary?'[90] The slogan appeared everywhere and in March 1944 was even adopted for a biscuit advertisement:

LONDON–OXFORD
– is the journey really necessary?

Not in war-time! Therefore, Macfarlane
Lang's Biscuits are not making the journey
but, Granola Digestive, Oval Osborne and
Somerset and other favourite biscuits will
be back in the shops when peace returns.[91]

The discouraging message was driven home by other measures, such as withdrawing Cheap Day Tickets in 1943; long-distance travellers, however, had no choice but to use the railways. Some trains in the Bicester area were so crammed with service personnel that passengers were forced to stand in the corridors, vestibules and even the toilet compartments.[92] The crowds at Oxford station at Whitsun in 1944 recalled pre-war Bank Holidays as war workers struggled to get home to their families.[93]

Increased military traffic, especially in the run-up to D-Day, led to some important railway improvements in the county, but these were not primarily designed for the convenience of the travelling public. The doubling of the line between Didcot and Newbury in 1942–3 did in fact cause serious dislocation

One goods train waits for another opposite Oxford North Goods Yard in 1943. The train on the left is heading on to the Bletchley line, utilizing a wartime connection made between the parallel GWR and LMS lines.

because all passenger and goods services had to be suspended for eight months.[94] On the Fairford branch a new passengers-only station was built at Carterton in 1944 to serve personnel at RAF Brize Norton.[95] Such benefits would scarcely have been evident to the average passenger travelling in a typically late and dirty train in the black-out; even the long-awaited arrival could be hazardous and in October 1940, for instance, J.F. Fulton arrived from Oxford in blacked out Cambridge as the air-raid sirens wailed:

> I was up near the engine of a long train and emerged in the yards beyond the end of the platform into the blackest night I ever hope to experience. After stumbling into railway trucks, switches, and a number of other hazards, I sat down for five minutes to get dark-adapted, and then stumbled along the platform looking for the exit, only to find myself before I knew it in the Ladies' Room. I beat a hasty retreat into a cage of poultry, and after catching my steel helmet on a motor bicycle I eventually found the bar and later the exit.[96]

For the private motorist, petrol rationing was introduced as early as 16 September 1939 because of the threat to supplies. Branded petrol was replaced by 'pool', a medium octane blend, and motorists were allocated a basic monthly ration which ranged from 4 gallons for a baby Austin to 10 gallons for a Rolls-Royce. Supplementary allowances could be claimed for extra domestic or business needs and from October 1940 for the Government's 'Help Your Neighbour' free lift scheme.[97] In November 1941 J.D. Mabbott of St John's College asked for extra petrol because he had to go to Cambridge and address a staff officers' course; he argued without too much conviction that he could return the same day if he travelled by car whereas he would have to stay overnight and return the next day if he used the train. The Divisional Petroleum Officer at Reading was impressed:

> Dear Sir
>
> Thank you for your letter of November 1st. In view of the special circumstances which you adduce (and moved, I must confess, by the fact that you are the only applicant who during the two years of Petrol Rationing has ever admitted that he had not a strong case!) I will arrange to make you the necessary issue.
>   If towards the 15th November you will be good enough to let me know the horse-power of your car, the registration number, and the mileage involved, I will have despatched to you the necessary coupons valid for December.[98]

Petrol for commercial vehicles was dyed red to prevent its illicit use by civilians, but people found ways of filtering out the dye and there was a flourishing black market if the motorist was prepared to pay the inflated price of about 6s 6d per gallon.[99] Another illegal option was to buy extra coupons, but this was a risky undertaking which cost one Oxford man a fine of £10 in January 1943.[100] As with other forms of rationing, measures to conserve petrol stocks spawned a large bureaucracy and surveillance could seem overbearing; in October 1943 a Wheatley woman was fined £3 after visiting the Churchill Hospital to make arrangements for an officer's family because she had misused petrol that had been issued for shopping and taking her children to school.[101]

A consignment of precious 'Pool' petrol comes to grief on the A40 near Eynsham in May 1941 after colliding with a lorry from South Wales.

Private motorists were understandably reluctant to take their cars off the road, and in February 1940 H. Stanley Askew of The County Garages wrote to the *Chipping Norton Advertiser* warning them to consider the cost and inconvenience of alternative transport and the threat to the railways from air raids.[102] The Government, too, resisted pressure to abolish the civilian petrol ration in 1941 for social and political reasons, but was forced to grasp the nettle as petrol and rubber supplies dwindled. From July 1942 most drivers had to drain their sumps and leave their cars on wood blocks in the garage for the rest of the war.[103] The pony and trap became a familiar sight again in Burford, and at Lyneham an Italian prisoner of war known as Tony fashioned a chariot out of an old tub and was often seen driving along like an ancient Roman charioteer. In the Wychwood villages,

> light carts appeared from nowhere, old traps were retrieved from the scrap heap; and floats, long thought to be worthless, suddenly became very valuable. One particularly interesting vehicle was a fine four-wheel dog-cart which made its appearance in Shipton. People who wanted to 'cut a dash' laid their cars aside and bought high dog-carts and smart new harness. . . . I saw a cart, made by an amateur, with pine logs and a couple of motor wheels. It served its purpose very well indeed. Many motor trailers had shafts fitted to them and were horse-drawn.

Curry's Ltd, in Banbury, stressed that it was patriotic to ride and buy a bike, while for many people 'Shanks's pony' assumed a renewed importance as the cheapest and most reliable way of travelling from A to B.[104]

Our Horses in Wartime .

Petrol rationing encouraged a return to horse-drawn transport. This drawing shows some of the vehicles that were used in the Wychwood villages.

Transport restrictions had further repercussions on everyday life because they seriously affected commercial deliveries. At Wootton near Woodstock, for example, lack of transport was viewed as 'probably our greatest inconvenience';

> The loss of our carrier early in the war was a major calamity. The visiting tradespeople, who came round regularly in their vans with fish, fruit and vegetables, the fish and chip van, the ice cream van, they all disappeared. There were no trade deliveries from Oxford, and our local shops in Woodstock and neighbouring places could only deliver once a week. Bread could only be delivered three times a week, milk must be fetched. The laundry van made rare and erratic appearances, sometimes at intervals of five to six weeks.[105]

In Oxford a new pooling system for deliveries was introduced in March 1942. The city was divided into six zones and each zone had a weekly delivery of loads weighing 28 lb or more; residents were expected to make their own arrangements to fetch any lighter packages.[106]

The cumulative effect of all these shortages and regulations was to make life gloomier at a time when individuals were already fearful for their own and their family's safety and, of course, anxious about the outcome of the war. On 6 July 1940 the Chief Constable of Oxford reported that four people had committed suicide in the past week because of war strain.[107] The annual report of Oxford's Park Hospital for functional nervous disorders in 1943 noted that:

> In the case of 23 patients war conditions played some part either direct or indirect in precipitating the illness. Separation of families, the effort to adapt to

strange conditions of work, long hours of duty, the emotional tension and physical hazards of air raids, the trials of shopping and travelling, and the many minor irritations inseparable from the fifth year of the war sometimes prove more than the person who is constitutionally predisposed to anxiety or depression can stand.[108]

Most people, however, found ways of coping with the stress and humour was one essential safety valve. A passenger on the crowded train from Paddington to Oxford on 1 September 1939 provided some examples:

There were jokes, some rude and crude, from members of the OBLI who filled the train on their way to Cowley Barracks. There was also the rich instinctive humour of the British race. The train was full. Soldiers lay in the corridor trying to snatch some sleep after a day's work and before a future they could not predict. One remarked, 'Well, the Polish Corridor will be better than this.' Another promised his wife one of Hitler's moustaches; another shouted, 'God bless the Fuehrer. I was going to get married next Saturday. I'm a free man now.'[109]

At Benson the chairman of the British Legion's Entertainments Committee, William Frankum, described the supreme sense of humour which infused all their efforts:

It could be seen, for instance, in the Home Guard where one old soldier Legionaire, who had been training strenuously for the expected invasion of England, chided Hitler for having gone the other way (against Russia). 'Waste of —— time,' he said!
In all the known (& unknown) ways and means of raising funds for Charity, humour was foremost; in Plays and Sketches, 'Colonels' would become Hangmen or ardent Lovers, while others of a less intelligent type would be raised to the Peerage; 'Fat Ladies' would try & look like Fairies, but after some good-humoured leg-pulling each would gradually regain his or her proper station in life.[110]

Morale was also boosted by a wide range of wartime entertainment. Popular songs encouraged people to 'Be Like the Kettle and Sing' and 'Keep Your Sunny Side Up'; Vera Lynn provoked tears with 'The White Cliffs of Dover' and Zoe Gail sang 'I'm Gonna Get Lit Up When the Lights Go Up in London'. There were also cheerful songs like 'We're Going to Hang Out Our Washing on the Siegfried Line' which had to be dropped hastily after the invasion of France, and wonderfully silly songs like 'Mairzy Doats' ('Mares eat oats . . . and little lambs eat ivy').[111] ENSA, the Entertainments National Service Association, had staged 900 popular concerts for troops and war workers in Oxfordshire by January 1944 and celebrities such as Arthur Askey and Gracie Fields starred at local venues in 1941. A lesser known wartime agency, CEMA or the Council for the Encouragement of Music and the Arts, encouraged and supported artistic excellence; its local beneficiaries included the Oxford Pilgrim Players, founded by Ruth Spalding, who toured the county in cars and vans and played in camps, hangars, halls and even air-raid shelters.[112]

In every community the wireless became a crucial focus for news, and people's spirits were raised by light entertainment programmes such as ITMA, 'It's That Man Again', with Tommy Handley; characters such as 'Funf', 'Colonel Chin-strap' and 'Ali Oop' were known to all and Mrs Mopp's 'Can I do you now, Sir?' became a national catch-phrase.[113] Other favourite programmes included 'Much Binding in the Marsh' and 'The Brains' Trust'; the latter was broadcast from the Dragon School in Oxford in 1944 and spawned imitations like the Oxford Brains' Trust held at the Wingfield-Morris Hospital, where a panel of local luminaries fielded questions from the patients.[114]

Despite the transport difficulties people flocked to local cinemas and theatres. Customers were reassured that the buildings were safe and at the Crown Cinema in Bicester, for example, there was 'plenty of room in a large cellar in time of air raids'; by November 1939 the Grand Theatre in Banbury had installed a steel inner roof between the auditorium ceiling and the asbestos outer roof:

> Patrons of the Grand may henceforth enjoy the programmes secure in the knowledge that their heads are protected by three (and in most cases four or five) roofings, including one of steel.[115]

The enthusiasm for film-going encouraged Oxford cinemas to consider opening on Sunday evenings, and in August 1940 local magistrates allowed them to do so provided that 25 per cent of their net profits were given to charity.[116] A similar arrangement was made in Bicester after the Crown Cinema burned down in July 1943 and the Regal was allowed to open on Sunday evenings if it contributed £5 to charity; by November there was sufficient demand for a third house and opening at 2.30 p.m., but the management decided to abandon Sunday opening after the magistrates asked for the charitable contribution to be raised to £20.[117]

With the closure of many London theatres, the New Theatre and the Oxford Playhouse attracted large audiences to see a veritable feast of high-class productions performed by well-known actors. At the New Theatre in February 1944 Beatrice Lillie and Robert Morley were appearing in the premiere of Morley's new comedy, *Staff Dance*; in September John Gielgud, Peggy Ashcroft and Leslie Banks were among the star-studded cast of *Hamlet*.[118] At the Playhouse the producer, Peter Ashmore, defied problems with 'man-power, materials, transport [late arrival of costumes or non-arrival of wigs was a constant bugbear] and the black-out' to provide productions which were, as Frank Dibb later recalled, 'remembered with both affection and excitement by those Oxford folk who saw them'.[119]

Oxford in wartime became an inland holiday resort, serving not only an enlarged local population but also people from further afield who were prevented from going to coastal towns. In August 1940 the city was crowded:

> The smaller hotels and boarding houses are full and the river is proving the most popular attraction. The steamer excursions are packed to capacity and those who hire out punts, canoes and rowing boats are doing a roaring trade – better than for many years. Shopkeepers are also finding the benefit of the increase in population, as also are the places of entertainment.[120]

Holidays at Home; local members of the Amalgamated Engineering Union make the best of a dreary summer's day on a Salter's steamer.

In that glorious summer the threat of invasion hardly seemed possible and users of the river had to be reminded that Defence Regulations even extended to their unattended rowing boats, punts and canoes:

> It is laid down that all oars, poles, paddles, rowlocks, rudders, painters, masts and sails shall be removed from the vessel.[121]

The summer entertainments provided in inland towns and cities were inevitably limited, however, and many people were still keen to go on holiday or, in the case of war workers, to return to their families. From 1942 the Government therefore encouraged local authorities to set up 'Holidays at Home' programmes which would serve to boost morale and, at the same time, discourage use of the overcrowded railways. Oxford's first experiment in 1942 had mixed success and Miss McGuire of the Town Clerk's Department argued that it 'did not apparently touch a very large proportion of the population'. Mrs Eleanor Butler of Crick Road had been affected against her will and wrote forcefully to the Town Clerk in April 1943:

> I want to put in a plea that residents in the areas adjacent to the Parks shall not again have to endure the awful noise they suffered from last year. A loud

speaker was installed in the Parks . . . and this relayed music and speech for seven hours every day except the last which fortunately was wet. The sound was so loud that it was impossible to concentrate on anything, and it wrecked work and relaxation alike. I and my neighbours were driven crazy by it. In this fourth year of the war when we are all suffering from the stress and strain, I do beg that we may be spared this extra trial to our nerves.

The city nevertheless went ahead with a six-week programme which was designed to 'bring the seaside to Oxford'. Twelve donkeys were purchased for children's rides at Cutteslowe and extra paddle boats were acquired for the boating lake at Hinksey Park. Butlin's Fun Fair attracted crowds to Botley Road Recreation Ground in late July and then moved to Florence Park. Mrs Butler's patience was probably tested by two National Fire service demonstrations in the University Parks when about 1,000 people were shown how not to put out a fire and saw firemen dressed as women playing a comic football match. A gala week at Florence Park featured the Blue Star Dance Band, the Good Companions Concert Party, the Sonia Pledge School of Dancing, a seaside carnival, country dancing, a talent contest and a tennis tournament. A swimming gala at Hinksey Pool on 12 August featured swimming races, diving for plates, water polo and a humorous interlude. Intellectual entertainments included a stunning series of concerts in which renowned artists such as Gerald Moore, Moura Lympany, Ida Haendal, Dennis Brain, Heddle Nash and Leon Goossens attracted large audiences to the Town Hall.[122]

A similar range of 'Holidays at Home' events was held in Banbury during the school holidays in 1943, and a correspondent to the *Banbury Advertiser* described the fortnight as

Magnificent! . . . It may even be that some who ventured on the hazardous and comfortless journey in order to get a change of air and scenery might even be sorry that they did so when they hear of the splendid time enjoyed by those who obeyed the Government dictates.[123]

For year-round recreation, local people had generally to rely on their own resources and organized a wide variety of entertainments, many of them designed to raise funds for the war effort. At Burford, for instance, a small group of musicians formed a string orchestra to keep their spirits up, performed locally and even made recordings for the BBC under the direction of Imogen Holst. The orchestra also assisted the 'Burford Buffoons', a concert party of local talent, which gave two performances in Burford and one in Stow-on-the-Wold. One of the musicians recalled:

It is curious how the mind retains unimportant detail: the weather was so cold that winter that the beer, brought to revive the players, was found to have frozen; this was so impressive a sight that to this day the event is spoken of as the 'Frozen Beer Concert'.[124]

Steeple Barton residents formed an amateur theatrical company called the Barton Revellers, which provided entertainments in the Mission Hall and raised

Staff from Starling's carpet warehouse in Castle Street, Oxford, celebrate a patriotic Christmas in 1944.

about £300 for charity.[125] At Ewelme a village variety show entitled 'Ewelme Parade' ran for four nights in the ARP room in 1942 during a week to raise funds for food parcels for prisoners of war; the week culminated with a Carnival Dance and a violin recital in the church by the world-famous artists Adila Fachiri and Jelly d'Aranyi.[126] Hanwell enjoyed an annual fête in the grounds of the castle which helped 'to keep up the public morale in the village' as well as providing an opportunity for fund-raising.[127]

A Riverside Lido was created at Benson by Mr C.F. Young in 1943 and swimming regattas were held there during Wings for Victory Week and Salute the Soldier Week as a fund-raising entertainment.[128] At Bicester County School Lord and Lady Bicester were among the crowd at an open-air boxing match for London evacuees in September 1940:

> The youngsters who performed in the ring were chiefly those who had boxed on similar occasions in Bicester before, and while there was little science in their display of the noble art, enthusiasm was not lacking, and all appeared well matched. From the spectators' point of view the most exciting bout among the boys was that in which L. Chamberlayne and Jarvis took part. These extremely

diminutive youngsters, one of whom was lifted into the ring with one hand by one of the seconds, went at it hammer and tongs in a flurry of gloves, to the great amusement of the onlookers.[129]

Very different entertainment was provided at Banbury in November 1940 when there was a well-attended concert in aid of the Banbury Air Defence Cadet Corps and '13 year old Phyllis Taylor responded generously to her encore to tap dancing'.[130]

Transport restrictions and the black-out curtailed some leisure pursuits, but reduced horizons did, in a sense, give people more time for simple pleasures. The Mounthill Rambling Club, for example, had to adjust to reduced bus services and the impossibility of hiring a coach, and concentrated its activities on local outings which could be over by nightfall.[131] With the absence of private cars on by-roads, cycling and walking in the countryside became a pleasure again, and in 1944 the *Oxford Mail* began a series of walks 'Around and About Oxford' compiled by S.P.B. Mais.[132] Reading enjoyed a revival as Castle's bookshop in Thame urged:

> To pass the time away – Read. . . . Literally hundreds of titles. Read them and pass them on to the troops.[133]

The City Librarian in Oxford advised people to 'Let books brighten your black-out', and in Banbury Mr G. Gibbard remarked that

> Amusements are few and difficult to get at these days, and I think people are returning to quiet reading at home, and I think that will be even more emphasised.[134]

In September 1940 the Faringdon branch of Berkshire County Library reopened after two years' closure, and a People's Library was established in Henley in 1944, attracting a membership of 1,755 adults and children by the end of September.[135] Adult education also flourished and in March 1944 Oxford University's Extra-Mural Studies Department reported that the annual number of tutorial classes had risen from 46 to 59 since the academic year 1938/9 and the number of students from 1,200 to over 1,900.[136]

Pursuit of the opposite sex was perhaps no more and no less popular in wartime, but the frenetic pace of life and uncertainties about the future weakened traditional patterns of behaviour. The inhabitants of a largely rural county suddenly found themselves sharing their lives with war workers, evacuees and thousands of servicemen and women, including many from overseas. They met socially in pubs and clubs and at dances which, as Doree Griffin recalled, had the power to attract Land Girls at the end of a long working day:

> We were invited to these RAF dances quite often and we used to go and change in the cloakroom, you know, we'd look quite respectable and go into the hall. You could always tell a LA girl, she'd be sitting on her hands you see – she didn't have her hands displayed.
>   At times we have ridden up in very bad weather – we used to tie our long dresses up under our coats with bits of baling string and we'd have our shoes in

An employees' dance at the De Havilland factory in Witney in the spring of 1944.

the saddle bag at the back and our wellingtons on our feet. We'd plod and we'd get on our bikes and we'd cycle up to what was the gun post (this was when we were invited to the RAF Mess dance), leave our bicycles, go in the cloakroom, take our wellies off, untie our binder twine and try and look respectable.[137]

A new freedom in sexual relations was reflected by explicit advertisements in local newspapers warning people about venereal disease. At the Radcliffe Infirmary the numbers attending the VD clinic rose dramatically from 3,380 in 1939 to a peak of 8,516 in 1943. The Medical Officer of Health's annual report for 1945 noted that

The excitement of V Days, the last fling of departing alien troops, the return of infected or suspected husbands, have sent forth waves of new patients to the clinic.[138]

In general, however, there was still an innocence abroad and women students in Oxford suffered unusually from a shortage of male undergraduates. They were reduced to 'trawling' in Blackwell's bookshop, a process which involved singling out a solitary male and taking an apparently avid interest in nearby books; he could take this as a definite hint that an invitation to coffee would not be refused.[139]

CHAPTER NINE

The War Ends

The end of the war was not entirely unexpected or unheralded, and at the Bartons

As soon as the news began to get really exciting, and to look as if the hostilities would soon come to an end in Europe, Mrs Fleming called a meeting to discuss VE night celebrations. From then onwards nightly practices were held in the Mission Hall of patriotic songs, and daily parties could be seen working feverishly on a giant bonfire up the Kidlington road. A wonderful effigy of Hitler (cleverly made by Mrs Cross at Church Farm) stuffed with Home Guard training expedients, was hoisted on to the top, a guard being posted outside for fear some wag would set it alight before the appointed hour.[1]

When victory over Germany was formally announced in the evening of 7 May 1945, the news released nearly six years of pent-up anxiety into next day's

VE-Day celebrations in Witney retain the rapt attention of all but a few of the spectators.

celebration of VE-Day (Victory in Europe). The Bartons 'went mad with joy and flags' and staged a fancy-dress torchlight procession to the site of the bonfire:

> The bonfire then was lit, and what a blaze! It could be seen for miles and miles. The heat was so great it was impossible to dance round it, so Old Lang Syne was sung in little groups. Small boys ran about with bangers and squibs, till at last, leaving Hitler to smoulder away, the party returned to the Mission Hall to resume their jollifications. Prizes were given for the best Victory Fancy Dress, and dancing went on well into the early hours of the morning. Hoarse from shouting, and with weary feet, we dragged ourselves home, but with a wonderful feeling of security. No more bombs, no more rockets, and, thank God, no more Hitler.[2]

At Burford a bonfire blazed on the Recreation Ground, searchlights in the area made 'V' for Victory signs in the night sky, a thanksgiving service was held in the church and a victory peal was rung on the church bells.[3] A children's party was held at Sutton near Stanton Harcourt and this developed into an impromptu dance when a corporal from the nearby airfield fetched his radiogram.[4] There was a bonfire on the Green at Kingham and revellers at Banbury Cross daubed Queen Victoria's statue with lipstick.[5] In Bicester

> Thousands of troops from the neighbouring camps came into the town on Tuesday, and there was a deep feeling of joy throughout the day. . . . At dusk considerable enthusiasm prevailed. Fireworks were discharged, and there were

Jack Fowler's motorcycle and supporting muscle power haul materials up Beacon Hill for Eynsham's VE-Day bonfire.

displays at the camps. A bonfire was lit on the Market Square and street dancing was freely indulged in here, as well as at the junction of Sheep St. and St John's St., where a piano was brought out, and outside 'The Star', Highfield, where music was supplied by Star Sound System.[6]

Mrs Warner, exhausted by years of work at Ascott-under-Wychwood post office with scarcely a day off, had decided to pack up and get married at the end of the war:

So I well remember where I was on Armistice Day – in Webbers shop in Oxford buying the material to make my wedding dress and bridesmaids dresses. Suddenly the bells of Oxford began to ring, and the people in the streets were yelling and cheering. Everyone in the shop ran to the windows to see what was happening. Peace at last![7]

Oxford celebrated with particular exuberance and in the Carfax area cars and vans were stopped and shaken and the contents of a baker's van were hurled into the air. Many girls wore red, white and blue ribbons in their hair and everywhere

Watched by mums, dads and a hopeful cat, excited children enjoy a street party in Blackfriars Road, Oxford, on 9 March 1945.

there were people singing, shouting and dancing in the streets. Shop windows were illuminated for the first time since September 1939 and buildings such as Magdalen College, St John's College and St Edward's School were floodlit. Impromptu street parties were held all over the city, and at the end of a torchlight procession Hitler's effigy was ceremoniously burned opposite the Martyrs' Memorial.[8] In many cases, people went wild with excitement and James Pickles, the future judge, admitted to losing his virginity in Christ Church after drunken celebrations round a fire at Carfax corner.[9] The Carfax bonfire yielded 13 cwt of scrap iron when the City Engineer's staff came to clear the remains of sixty-three bonfires from the streets of Oxford.[10] Particular scenes lingered in the mind of one *Oxford Mail* journalist:

> A score or more young people playing 'oranges and lemons' on the roof of the air raid shelter in Broad-street.
>   A line of men and girls, arms linked, 'sweeping' the pavement so that one had to duck.
>   Another procession with the 'outriders' carrying hurricane lamps obtained from heaven knows where.
>   And what were the songs? Popular tunes of to-day and yesterday – things like 'Pistol-packin' Momma', 'Tipperary'. I heard only one 'patriotic' song – 'Boys of the Bulldog Breed'.[11]

Ron Smith, a resident of Oliver Road in Cowley and an employee at Pressed Steel, saw the flags of the Allies unfurled from the flagstaffs on the roof of the company offices, enjoyed the bonfires and good humour of the city centre and commented:

> Flags began to appear everywhere – and the one most humorous display I saw was in my street when a 'well adorned' string of highly coloured garments were suspended from two opposite houses and captioned 'Hitler's impregnable line'. What the line contained is not for me to say – but I was unaware that ladies did actually prefer such gaily coloured articles of clothing. VE plus one seemed to be devoted everywhere to kiddies celebrations – and where the elders did manage to obtain the provisions from I cannot imagine. Every street was bedecked – and the daubing of 'No Road' or 'Road Closed' made it evident that no interference was allowed in the kiddies assemblies.[12]

Everyone shared the general delight of VE-Day, but for many people the safe return of loved ones provided an additional thrill. At Coneygree Terrace in Chipping Norton, for example, Mrs Stokes received this letter from her son, Sgt. Norman Stokes, who had been shot down over Germany in November 1941 and had spent three and a half years in prisoner of war camps:

> My dearest Mother, Geraldine and all at Chippy,

> I can still hardly believe it, but it's really not a dream; I AM FREE! Allied forces caught up with us yesterday and now we are behind the lines in safe hands. We are told we might be flown back to England, so within a few days I should be seeing you again. Can you imagine that meeting? God – how I've longed for it.

Fun for all in Glanville Road, Oxford, as a bonfire blazes behind the 'conga' dancers; this was one of sixty-three street bonfires in the city on VE-Day.

Am too excited and full to write more now, so for the present we leave you. I can truly say it won't be long now. Get that whisky and plum pudding ready. Till we meet, love.

Ever your old Mowbray.[13]

One hundred days later, on 16 August 1945, the country was celebrating VJ-Day (Victory in Japan) and the end of hostilities throughout the world. Bicester folk enjoyed torchlight processions, bonfires, children's sports and fancy-dress parades, and ignored the discomfort of a rough surface to dance in the Market Square; fireworks lit up the skies around RAF Bicester and the Ordnance Depot. At Kirtlington a thanksgiving service in the church and a victory peal on the church bells was followed by a bonfire on the green at 10 p.m. and merrymaking until after midnight.[14] Chipping Norton entered enthusiastically into the spirit of VJ-Day:

At 4 p.m. children's dancing and community singing was held in the Town Hall and was extremely well patronised. This was followed by a military display and further community singing in the Market Square led by Councillor Swann. At 8 p.m. dancing came into its own once more, and an hour later the King's speech was relayed by loudspeakers fixed to the top of the Town Hall. More dancing followed, and the evening closed with a most impressive torchlight procession . . . to the Common, where a large bonfire was formally lit by the

Crowds in Chipping Norton Market Square attending the thanksgiving service which was held on Wednesday 15 August 1945.

Mayor and Mayoress (Councillor and Mrs Edgar Smith). The festivities continued to the early hours, but the public throughout was extremely well behaved and the police were not troubled in any way.[15]

At Crowmarsh Battle Farm in Benson, by contrast, harvesting was in full swing and F.P. Chamberlain noted that work simply continued as usual. There was no great excitement, just great thankfulness that no more young lives would be lost. At 10 p.m., however,

> four of us drove around on the hill etc – a few bonfires in the distance – a quiet nice night – spoke to the village policeman and others – a very pleasant atmosphere all felt an inside glow of pleasure that 'War Over'.[16]

Everywhere, the fund-raising effort was diverted towards returning servicemen and women. At Kingham a 'Welcome Home Fund' raised £732 10s,[17] and the people of Blackthorn raised £55 7s 4d by holding a 'Welcome Home' Sports in Mr Newell's field on 18 August.[18] New names had to be added to countless war memorials and the country faced years of austerity, but there was real hope for a better future as eleven-year-old L.H. Connor had foreseen at Bignell Park Evacuated School:

Children from The Leys in Chipping Norton pose with their mothers before tucking into their VJ-Day tea.

AFTER THE WAR

> After this war is over,
> We will rejoice in clover.
> The buildings will be replaced,
> The builders will make haste.
>
> After this war is over,
> Guns will not fire at Dover.
> Lord Woolton will not ration,
> Things will come back in fashion.
>
> After this war is over,
> The people will not be sober.
> The lights of London will shine again,
> And the sirens unheeded can wail in vain.[19]

Notes

Abbreviations

BanA	*Banbury Advertiser*
BG	*Banbury Guardian*
BicA	*Bicester Advertiser*
Bodl	Bodleian Library
CNA	*Chipping Norton Advertiser*
COS	Centre for Oxfordshire Studies
FA	*Faringdon Advertiser*
HS	*Henley Standard*
IWM	Imperial War Museum
NBH	*North Berks Herald*
OA	Oxfordshire Archives
OCA	Oxford City Archives
OHA	Oral History Archive
OM	*Oxford Mail*
OPA	Oxfordshire Photographic Archive
ORCC	Oxfordshire Rural Community Council
OT	*Oxford Times*
PRO	Public Record Office
TG	*Thame Gazette*
WG	*Witney Gazette*
WLWO	'When The Lights Went Out' exhibition

Chapter One
1. OM 3.9.1939
2. OM 4.9.1939
3. BG 7.9.1939
4. COS Lloyd Papers
5. OM 4.9.1939
6. COS OHA Tape 32
7. COS Lloyd Papers
8. OM 3.9.1939, 4.9.1939
9. BicA 8.9.1939
10. OM 4.9.1939
11. BG 7.9.1939
12. *Berkshire and Oxfordshire Advertiser* 8.9.1939; OM 4.9.1939
13. WG 8.9.1939
14. BicA 8.9.1939

Chapter Two
1. OA Report ARP Organizing Committee, 13.5.1936
2. OM 3.4.1939
3. OCA CC.1.2. ARP Committee Minute Book 1938–9, pp. 91–6
4. Oxfordshire County Council Reports 11.5.1938, pp. 115–18; ibid. 8.11.1939, p. 23
5. OM 22.6.1939
6. COS G. Fray, ed., *Current Events and Wartime Benson* (1946), p. 148
7. *It Happened in the Dorn Valley* (1946), p. 8
8. NBH 25.8.1939, 8.9.1939
9. OM 25.8.1939, 26.8.1939, 31.8.1939; Sir Edmund Craster, *History of the Bodleian Library 1845–1945* (1952), pp. 341–2
10. OM 2.9.1939
11. NBH 8.9.1939
12. BicA 8.9.1939
13. COS *Warbling Notes* 2 (Dec 1939)
14. OM 28.8.1939; BicA 8.9.1939
15. COS *Warbling Notes* 2 (Dec 1939)
16. BanA 28.9.1939; BicA 17.11.1939
17. CNA 15.12.1939; OM 13.9.1939
18. OM 20.10.1939
19. *Evacuees and Bicester* (1979), p. 14
20. Bodl MS Top Oxon e 289, p. 7
21. OM 8.3.1940
22. OCA City Engineer's Dept Newscuttings, 1939–42, p. 40
23. COS Fray, op. cit., p. 10
24. OM 9.11.1939
25. OA CCC 1121
26. *American Oxonian* (April 1941), p. 74
27. CNA 8.12.1939
28. E. Fairfax, *Calling All Arms* (1945), p. 65
29. W.R. Nicholson, *Here and There* (1974), p. 7
30. *Country Life* 28.12.1945; COS WLWO 96
31. *Record of Witney* 11 (1980), p. 15
32. COS WLWO 96
33. CNA 8.9.1939

34. OM 2.9.1939; NBH 8.9.1939, 20.9.1939
35. *Record of Witney* 2(3) (1990)
36. FA 28.6.1940, 12.7.1940, 9.8.1940, 23.8.1940
37. COS OHA Tape 32; OPA 80/9959, 10115
38. COS WLWO 3
39. OM 22.9.1939
40. TG 5.9.1939
41. OM 2.7.1940
42. OM 8.7.1940
43. COS Pamphlet OXFO 944.4
44. OM 22.8.1942
45. COS WLWO 18
46. COS WLWO 72
47. CNA 8.9.1939
48. CNA 7.3.1940; COS *Warbling Notes* 3 (Jan 1940); FA 22.3.1940
49. BicA 8.10.1943
50. *Evacuees and Bicester*, p. 14; OCA City Engineer's Dept Newscuttings, 1939–42, p. 3
51. *Safety First* (Nov 1940)
52. COS WLWO 5
53. OM 27.10.1939
54. NBH 13.10.1939
55. CNA 22.12.1939; TG 26.12.1939
56. OA T/SL 67(iii), p. 136
57. OM 14.11.1940
58. OM 9.10.1939
59. OA CCC 1121
60. BG 10.10.1940
61. Banbury Library Case E49; William Potts, *History of Banbury* (2nd edn, 1978), pp. 327–8
62. WG 29.11.1940
63. COS Fray, op. cit., p. 30
64. E.J. Lainchbury, *Kingham: The Beloved Place* (1957), p. 237
65. OA CCC 1121
66. *Safety First* (Nov 1940)
67. COS Fray, op. cit., p. 197; *Wychwoods History* 8 (1993), p. 8
68. Ibid., pp. 22, 121
69. Bodl MS Top Oxon e 289, p. 88
70. OM 6.2.1941; OA Misc | Lloyds I | 1
71. OCA Fire Service Record Book 3.5.1941; COS WLWO 96
72. Bodl MS Top Oxon e 289, p. 104
73. OA Emergency Civil Defence Committee, 2.10.1942
74. Craster, op. cit., pp. 342–3
75. COS Fray, op. cit., p. 148
76. M.J.F. Bowyer, *Action Stations: Military Airfields of Oxfordshire* (1988), p. 151
77. T.H. O'Brien, Civil Defence (1955), p. 431
78. OA Air Raid Log-book 1940–4; Bowyer, op. cit., p. 63
79. COS WLWO 105
80. Burford and Fulbrook WI, *Burford in the War of 1939–1945* (1947), p. 43; COS ORCC 68; Lainchbury, op. cit., pp. 252–3
81. Burford and Fulbrook WI, op. cit., p. 50; OM 10.5.1945; OCA Mayor of Oxford's Scrapbook 1939/40, p. 103
82. OA CCC 1099
83. Bodl MS Top Oxon c 474, p. 22
84. *Wootton: A Record of the War, 1939–1945* (1946), p. 2
85. *Dorn Valley*, p. 18
86. Bodl MS Top Oxon c 474, p. 26
87. OM 7.4.1943; BicA 8.10.1943
88. TG 23.7.1940
89. OM 25.9.1941
90. OA CCC 1136
91. HS 22.9.1944; COS Fray, op. cit., p. 286; OM 6.1.1945
92. COS WLWO 11
93. HS 22.9.1944
94. COS Fray, op. cit., p. 101

Chapter Three
1. Oxford City Council, *Government Evacuation Scheme, 1939–41* (1941), passim; NBH 29.12.1939
2. CNA 8.9.1939
3. COS OHA MT 968
4. CNA 8.9.1939
5. NBH 8.9.1939; CNA 8.9.1939; *Evacuees and Bicester* (1977), p. 13
6. OM 2.9.1939
7. OM 3.9.1939
8. OM 2.9.1939
9. COS OHA MT 968
10. *Woodcote in the War Years* (c. 1946), p. 3; COS G. Fray, ed., *Current Events and Wartime Benson* (1946), p. 152
11. OA P3 | 1 | A10 | 1
12. Charlbury WI, *Charlbury War Record* (1946), p. 5
13. OM 6.9.1939; OA County Evacuation Reports, 1939–41
14. Bodl MS Top Oxon e 289, p. 5
15. COS OHA MT 2506
16. OM 5–6.9.1939
17. CNA 29.9.1939
18. Burford and Fulbrook WI, *Burford in the War of 1939–1945* (1947), p. 59
19. BicA 8.9.1939
20. COS OHA VT 54
21. FA 26.7.1940
22. Ralph Blumenau, *A History of Malvern College, 1865–1965* (1965), pp. 125–32
23. Charlbury WI, op. cit., pp. 8–9
24. *Oxford Monthly* (Oct 1939); OM

7.9.1939; *Illustrated London News*, 11.11.1939

25. OM 28.8.1939; BicA 23.1.1980
26. Ronald Tree, *When the Moon was High* (1975), pp. 130–1; M.J.F. Bowyer, *Action Stations: Military Airfields of Oxfordshire* (1988), p. 114
27. CNA 6.10.1939
28. OA T/SL 101(ii); T/SL 58(ii)
29. *Record of Witney* 22 (1989); Bodl MS Top Oxon e 289, p. 81
30. OA T/SL 11(i)
31. CNA 13.10.1939; OT 19.7.1940
32. OA CCC 1182
33. Berkshire County Council, *Annual Report of the Medical Officer of Health* (1940), p. 11
34. OA P3|1|A10
35. OM 22.9.1939
36. Burford and Fulbrook WI, op. cit., p. 60
37. CNA 18.1.1940, 8.2.1940
38. BicA 21.6.1940
39. A.H. Symonds, *Havens Across the Sea* (1992), pp. 1, 8–9
40. COS WLWO 85
41. OM 21.9.1940; Bodl MS Top Oxon e 289, p. 72
42. Bodl MS Top Oxon e 289, p. 72; Oxford City Council, *Government Evacuation Scheme, 1939–41* (1941), pp. 4–5
43. Oxford City Council Reports 1940, p. 630
44. Vera Brittain, *England's Hour* (1981), pp. 165–6
45. OCA Mayor of Oxford's Scrapbook, 1940/1, p. 54
46. FA 27.9.1940
47. BanA 18.9.1940
48. TG 5.11.1940
49. Oxfordshire County Council, *Medical Officer of Health Reports, 1939–40*
50. COS Fray, op. cit., p. 281
51. Oxon MOH Reports, 1941–3
52. OA CCC 1121
53. OM 4.8.1941; BicA 3.12.1943
54. OA CCC 331
55. OM 10.7.1944; HS 28.7.1944
56. OM 14.7.1944
57. *Record of the War Activities of the Inhabitants of Leafield* (1948?), pp. 4–5
58. COS OHA 783
59. Barnett House, *London Children in Wartime Oxford* (1947), pp. 28–31
60. Oxon MOH Report, 1939
61. *It Happened in the Dorn Valley* (1946), p. 69
62. COS OHA MT 2506: OA P3|A10|1
63. BicA 12.4.1940
64. *Woodcote*, p. 4; BicA 7.9.1939
65. *Evacuees and Bicester*, p. 25

66. NBH 8.12.1944
67. OA CCC 1241
68. COS WLWO 95
69. *Evacuees and Bicester*, p. 23
70. Barnett House, op. cit., p. 80
71. OA CCC 1241
72. CNA 20.6.1940
73. *Evacuees and Bicester*, p. 23
74. OM 9.11.1939
75. CNA 22.5.1941
76. OA P3|1|A10|1
77. NBH 4.10.1940
78. OCA Mayor of Oxford's Scrapbook 1939/40, p. 85
79. Bodl MS Top Oxon e 289, p. 73
80. Ibid., p. 106
81. NBH 4.10.1940; OT 24.1.1941
82. OA P3|1|A10|1
83. Charlbury WI, op. cit., p. 6
84. OCA DD.1.13 Evacuation Committee Minute Book 1939–42, p. 65
85. OA County Emergency Committee for Civil Defence, 1942–5
86. OM 17.10.1940
87. OM 25.9.1939; CNA 25.12.1941
88. OM 19.2.1943; Barnett House, op. cit., p. 80
89. BicA 15.10.1943

Chapter Four
1. *Record of the War Activities of the Inhabitants of Leafield* (1948?), p. 9
2. *Oxfordshire and Buckinghamshire Infantry Light Infantry War Chronicle* [hereafter *War Chronicle*] 1 (1939–40), pp. 35, 82
3. A.H.T. Robb-Smith, *A Short History of the Radcliffe Infirmary* (1970), pp. 175, 177
4. Charlbury WI, *Charlbury War Record* (1946), p. 18; E.J. Lainchbury, *Kingham: The Beloved Place* (1957), p. 232
5. TG 16.7.1940; FA 19.1.1940
6. FA 26.4.1940
7. M.J.F. Bowyer, *Action Stations: Military Airfields of Oxfordshire* (1988), pp. 7–8
8. OM 20.10.1939
9. NBH 24.11.1939; 5.4.1940
10. TG 14.5.1940
11. OM 1.6.1940
12. COS OHA Tape 32
13. *War Chronicle* 1 (1939–40), pp. 94–6; OCA Mayor of Oxford's Scrapbook 1939/40, p. 226
14. COS WLWO M1; COS G. Fray, ed., *Current Events and Wartime Benson* (1946), p. 269
15. St John's College MS, History of College Farm, Long Wittenham, 1932–60, vol. 1, p. 200

16. COS WLWO M1
17. *Country Life* 20.9.1990
18. OCA GG.4.6. Special Committees Minute Book, 1939–42, pp. 74, 83; COS Fray, op. cit., p. 30
19. WG 12.7.1940
20. FA 13.9.1940; COS WLWO 104
21. Burford and Fulbrook WI, *Burford in the War of 1939–1945* (1947), p. 27; COS Fray, op. cit., p. 281; OM 4.1.1944
22. TG 8.10.1940
23. TG 27.8.1940; COS Fray, op. cit., p. 128; NBH 28.6.1940
24. Bowyer, op. cit., pp. 8, 114, 134–5, 148
25. OA CCC 1121
26. Bowyer, op. cit., pp. 48–9
27. Charlbury WI, op. cit., p. 3
28. WG 19.7.1940; *War Chronicle* 2 (1940–2), pp. 97–8
29. Charlbury WI, op. cit., p. 3
30. BicA 1.3.1940; COS Pamphlet 920 SOLF
31. COS OHA Tape 76; OA CCC 1121
32. Bodl MS Top Oxon e 289, p. 43
33. WG 31.5.1940
34. BicA 5.7.1940; W.R. Nicholson, *Here and There* (1974), p. 9
35. CNA 5.9.1940; TG 10.9.1940
36. Bowyer, op. cit., passim
37. COS Fray, op. cit., p. 81
38. Bowyer, op. cit., p. 77
39. COS Fray, op. cit., pp. 41–2, 77, 284
40. *Woodcote in the War Years* (c. 1946), p. 16
41. *Eynsham Record* 8 (1991), p. 42
42. COS Fray, op. cit., p. 81; *Wootton: A Record of the War 1939–1945* (1946), p. 2
43. Bowyer, op. cit., pp. 17, 27, 43, 92, 135; NBH 15.11.1940
44. Nicholson, op. cit., p. 6
45. Bowyer, op. cit., pp. 94, 122, 140
46. COS Fray, op. cit., p. 97
47. Judy and Stuart Dewey, *The Book of Wallingford* (1977), p. 134
48. Bowyer, op. cit., pp. 150–1
49. Ibid., p. 27; COS Fray, op. cit., p. 80
50. COS Fray, op. cit., pp. 111–12
51. Ibid., pp. 80, 94; Bowyer, op. cit., pp. 30, 72, 112
52. E.A. Lawton and M.W. Sackett, *Bicester Military Railway* (1992), pp. 13–20; *50 years of COD Bicester and Bicester Garrison 1942–1992* (1992), pp. 7–8, 14; BicA 9.7.1980
53. Charlbury WI, op. cit., pp. 18–19
54. Lainchbury, op. cit., p. 239
55. Paul Karau, Mike Parsons and Kevin Robertson, *The Didcot, Newbury and Southampton Railway* (1981), pp. 43–8;

R.A. Cooke, *Track layout diagrams . . . Section 23 (1976)*, p. 20
56. COS Fray, op. cit., p. 281
57. Ibid., p. 70; PRO WO 199|816; IWM photographs e.g. H27843, 27922, 27933, 28016; R.L. Collison, *The Cutteslowe Walls* (1963), p. 127
58. Burford and Fulbrook WI, op. cit., p. 17
59. Ibid., p. 18; Bowyer, op. cit., pp. 62–3
60. Charlbury WI, op. cit., p. 26
61. Robb-Smith, op. cit., pp. 171, 182, 187; OM 27.7.1944
62. Bowyer, op. cit., pp. 63, 95, 101; *Record of Witney* 5 (1978), p. 10
63. COS Fray, op. cit., p. 286
64. *War Chronicle* 4 (1944–5), pp. 48–71
65. Bowyer, op. cit., pp. 63, 95
66. Charlbury WI, op. cit., p. 3
67. War Chronicle 4 (1944–5), pp. 77–8
68. Bowyer, op. cit., pp. 64–5, 97; COS Fray, op. cit., p. 286
69. COS WLWO 96; BicA 3.4.1975
70. COS OHA Tapes 73, 75
71. COS WLWO M15
72. COS OHA Tape 74
73. COS Fray, op. cit., p. 120
74. *War Chronicle* 1 (1939–40), p. 35
75. OA CCC 1248
76. OA CCC 1241; National Trust, *Basildon Park, Berkshire* (1989), p. 14
77. Philip Larkin, *Jill* (1946), p. 100; *Wootton* p. 2
78. Burford and Fulbrook WI, op. cit., p. 27; COS OPA 80/9970
79. *Record of Eynsham* 7 (1990), p. 36
80. HS 2.6.1944
81. BicA 30.7.1943; 25.2.1944
82. CNA 12.8.1943
83. OA CCC 1121: BicA 24.9.1943
84. COS OHA Tape 32; *Record of Witney* 5 (1978), p. 11
85. COS WLWO 6,23
86. CNA 18.11.1943
87. OM 25.1.1944
88. *War Chronicle* 3 (1942–4), p. 53
89. CNA 10.2.1944
90. Charlbury WI, op. cit., p. 26
91. OM 29.3.1944
92. BicA 17.8.1945
93. COS OHA MT783
94. OM 21.6.1940; OCA Mayor of Oxford's Scrapbook 1939/40, p. 103
95. OM 25.1.1944, 10.5.1945
96. OM 21.6.1940; IWM Photographs D191110, 19112–23, 191147
97. OCA Mayor of Oxford's Scrapbook 1939/40, pp. 65, 103
98. OA CCC 1121
99. OM 12.9.1944

100. BicA 17.9.1943
101. COS Fray, op. cit., pp. 214–17
102. OM 13.9.1944
103. *Woodcote*, pp. 1–2; T.B. Scotcher, *An English Village in Wartime* (1945), pp. 3–4, 30
104. COS WLWO 40
105. COS WLWO 12
106. BicA 16.7.1943
107. COS WLWO 71
108. OM 26.6.1944
109. CNA 6.5.1943, 30.11.1943; *Eynsham Record* 7 (1990), p. 37
110. OM 11.9.1944
111. OA T/SL 67(iii), 177

Chapter Five
1. *Record of service: the 'Highlands' Platoon* (1945?), p. 3
2. Ibid.; BanA 15.5.40
3. BicA 17.5.40
4. *Story of the 1st Berks (Abingdon) Battalion Home Guard* (1945), p. 23
5. OM 27.11.44
6. TG 1.10.40; OCA Mayor of Oxford's Scrapbook 1939/40, p. 216
7. Burford and Fulbrook WI, *Burford in the War of 1939–1945* (1947), pp. 32–3: *Story of the 1st Berks*, p. 27
8. *Story of the 1st Berks*, p. 10; N. Longmate, *The Real Dad's Army* (1974), p. 45
9. OCA Mayor of Oxford's Scrapbook 1939/40, p. 212
10. *Woodcote in the War Years* (c. 1946), p. 5; E.J. Lainchbury, *Kingham: The Beloved Place* (1957), pp. 243–4; information from Jim Barnes, Shipton-under-Wychwood
11. *Story of the 1st Berks*, p. 10
12. Lainchbury, op. cit., p. 246; OM 9.8.40; *Story of the 1st Berks*, p. 62
13. Longmate, op. cit., p. 45
14. *Allen's Activities* 18 (1953), p. 7
15. OA CCC 1127
16. W.R. Nicholson, *Here and There* (1974), p. 10
17. COS G. Fray, ed., *Current Events and Wartime Benson* (1946), pp. 182, 267–9
18. A.S.T. Fisher, *The History of Westwell* (1972), p. 117
19. TG 1.10.40
20. *Eynsham Record* 7 (1990), pp. 39–41
21. Nicholson, op. cit., p. 10; *Record of service*, p. 6
22. *It Happened in the Dorn Valley* (1946), p. 26; Bodl MS Top Oxon e 766, p. 99
23. TG 23.7.40; Lainchbury, op. cit., pp. 245, 248
24. *Story of the 1st Berks*, p. 11
25. Ibid., p. 24; Burford and Fulbrook WI, op. cit., p. 33

26. *Dorn Valley*, p. 27
27. *Story of the 1st Berks*, p. 11
28. *Dorn Valley*, p. 27
29. *Record of service*, p. 9
30. COS WLWO M26
31. *Dorn Valley*, pp. 27–8; *Story of the 1st Berks*, p. 24; *Record of service*, pp. 4–5, 10–11; COS WLWO M26
32. Lainchbury, op. cit., p. 244
33. Nicholson, op. cit., p. 10
34. Burford and Fulbrook WI, op. cit., p. 13
35. *Dorn Valley*, p. 68
36. *Story of the 1st Berks*, pp. 25, 60–1
37. *Record of service*, p. 17
38. COS WLWO M26
39. Lainchbury, op. cit., p. 251; *Story of the 1st Berks*, p. 17
40. *Record of service*, pp. 11–12
41. *Story of the 1st Berks*, p. 53
42. OM 3.3.43
43. Lainchbury, op. cit., p. 257; *Record of the War Activities of the Inhabitants of Leafield* (1948?), p. 6
44. Lainchbury, op. cit., p. 249
45. CNA 24.4.41
46. OM 16.6.1942; COS WLWO M26
47. Lainchbury, op. cit., p. 249; *Record of service*, pp. 19–21
48. BicA 12.8.43; OM 16.2.43
49. *Record of service*, pp. 20–1
50. Lainchbury, op. cit., p. 258; COS WLWO M26
51. *Dorn Valley*, pp. 30–3

Chapter Six
1. E. Fairfax, *Calling All Arms* (1945), pp. 15, 128; P.W.S. Andrews and Elizabeth Brunner, *The Life of Lord Nuffield* (1959), p. 232
2. CNA 20.10.1939
3. Andrews and Brunner, op. cit., pp. 233–4
4. *City Motors During the War 1939–1945* (1945?), p. 3
5. Bodl MS Top Oxon e 289, p. 11
6. Fairfax, op. cit., pp. 16, 24, 26, 31–4; COS OHA Tape 32; OM 29.8.1944, 2.9.1944
7. *Record of Witney* 11 (1980), pp. 8–9, 13; De Havilland (Witney) Association, *Witney Memorial Folder* (1980), p. 4
8. Fairfax, op. cit., p. 26
9. Ibid., pp. 34, 39
10. COS WLWO War Work 34
11. Fairfax, op. cit., pp. 38–40
12. Ibid., pp. 44–5
13. Ibid., pp. 121, 128–37
14. OM 23.5.1945; COS Howse Collection 1.10
15. Fairfax, op. cit., pp. 148–50

16. Ibid., pp. 143–6
17. BanA 18.5.1939
18. William Potts, *History of Banbury* (2nd edn., 1978), p. 328
19. Ibid., p. 329; Banbury Library Case B 45A
20. E.J. Lainchbury, *Kingham: The Beloved Place* (1957), p. 236
21. Alfred Plummer and R.E. Early, *The Blanket Makers* (1969), p. 132; OA B1|C6|3
22. *Record of Witney* 11 (1980), p. 10
23. Bodl MS Top Oxon d 484, p. 147
24. *Allen's Activities* 18 (1953), pp. 5, 8–15
25. Peter Sutcliffe, *The Oxford University Press: An Informal History* (1978), pp. 249–52
26. *American Oxonian* (April 1941), p. 89
27. *Oxfordshire Local History* 4 (1992), pp. 16–18
28. *Woodcote in the War Years* (*c.* 1946), p. 10
29. OM 20.11.1943
30. *Isis* 11.5.1949
31. OM 17.7.1940
32. Bodl MS Top Oxon e 289, pp. 34–5, 84
33. *City Motors*, pp. 3, 5–6, 8
34. HS 14.4.1944
35. OA B7|X|9
36. CNA 11.2.1943
37. Fairfax, op. cit., p. 146
38. *It Happened in the Dorn Valley* (1946), p. 60
39. OM 15.3.1941
40. OM 27.9.1941
41. OM 29.10.1941
42. COS Howse Collection 1.6–7
43. *Allen's Activities* 18 (1953), p. 11
44. De Havilland Assoc., op. cit., p. 12
45. OM 12.9.1942
46. OM 1.2.1941, 16/17.12.1940
47. *Record of Witney* 11 (1980), p. 9; COS OHA Tape 32
48. OM 12.10.1940
49. OT 1.11.1940, 22.11.1940
50. OM 24.4.1942
51. OM 17.3.1943; Oxford City Council Reports 1942/3, p. 100
52. OM 29.7.1943
53. OA CCC 329
54. CNA 28.3.1940
55. COS G. Fray, ed., *Current Events and Wartime Benson* (1946), p. 64
56. OM 16.5.1942
57. COS Fray, op. cit., pp. 69–70
58. OM 24.2.1943
59. HS 21.4.1944
60. COS Fray, op. cit., pp. 64–5
61. PRO MAF|32|911|147
62. COS Fray, op. cit., p. 64
63. Malcolm Graham and Melanie Williams, *When the Lights Went Out: Oxfordshire, 1939–1945* (1979), p. 19; A.F. Martin and R.W. Steel, *The Oxford Region* (1954), p. 135; R.A. Cooke, *Track layout diagrams . . .* Section 27 (1987), p. 15; *Journal of the Royal Agricultural Society* 110 (1949), p. 4
64. OM 16.8.1940, 17.7.1940
65. CNA 4.9.1941
66. CNA 2.9.1943
67. COS Fray, op. cit., pp. 39–40
68. FA 26.4.1940; CNA 30.9.1943
69. COS WLWO M20; St John's College MS, History of College Farm, Long Wittenham, 1932–60, vol. 1, p. 167
70. COS OHA MT 2506
71. COS OHA Tape 82
72. Burford and Fulbrook WI, *Burford in the War of 1939–1945* (1947), pp. 45–6
73. Graham and Williams, op. cit., p. 19
74. COS OHA Tape 80
75. COS OHA MT 2506
76. COS OHA Tape 79
77. COS OHA Tape 83
78. COS Fray, op. cit., p. 63
79. COS OHA Tapes 78–9; CNA 11.12.1941
80. COS Fray, op. cit., p. 70; OM 16.5.1942
81. OA CCC 1209
82. COS OHA Tapes 82–3
83. A.S.T. Fisher, *Westwell, Oxfordshire* (1972), p. 119
84. Graham and Williams, op. cit., p. 20
85. TG 16.7.1940
86. *Evacuees and Bicester* (1977), p. 17
87. *City of Oxford High School for Boys Magazine War Edition* 2 (December 1940), p. 10; 4 (April 1943), p. 22
88. OA T/SL 11(i)
89. Muriel Groves, *Records of Milton and Shipton-under-Wychwood during the War* (1948), p. 16
90. CNA 24.6.1943
91. NBH 13.10.1939; *COHS Magazine* 3 (December 1941), p. 11
92. OM 19.7.1940
93. OM 9.11.1940
94. OM 24.8.1940
95. OM 24.1.1940, 14.1.1942
96. Graham and Williams, op. cit., p. 20
97. OM 29.7.1940, 15.3.1941, 22.7.1942
98. OM 2.10.1940
99. OM 10.3.1943
100. OCA Mayor of Oxford's Scrapbook 1939/40, p. 39
101. COS Fray, op. cit., pp. 236–41
102. Ministry of Information, *Cotswold Club* (1943): copy of film owned by Rosemary Arnold, Deddington
103. OM 2.10.1940

104. Charlbury WI, *Charlbury War Record* (1946), p. 16
105. OA Baldons Produce Guild papers
106. OM 14.9.1940
107. OM 18.9.1940
108. OA T/SL 67(iii)
109. HS 4.2.1944
110. COS ORCC File 68
111. Charlbury WI, op. cit., p. 16; Groves, op. cit., p. 4
112. T.B. Scotcher, *A Village in Wartime* (1945), p. 23
113. Burford and Fulbrook WI, op. cit., p. 44
114. Charlbury WI, op. cit., pp. 13, 20
115. *Record of the War Activities of the Inhabitants of Leafield* (1948?), p. 8
116. OM 11.7.1940
117. *Oxford Monthly* (Sept 1940); COS WLWO 65
118. *Voluntary Organizations of the Country-side 1942/3* (1943), p. 2
119. COS Fray, op. cit., p. 158; *Record of Leafield*, p. 8
120. OM 19.1.1945
121. COS ORCC File 68
122. OCA Town Clerk's Correspondence
123. Penny Junor, *Burton: The Man Behind the Myth* (1985), p. 28; Humphrey Carpenter, *J.R.R. Tolkien* (1977), p. 193; Humphrey Carpenter, ed., *The Letters of J.R.R. Tolkien* (1981), p. 47
124. Sir Edmund Craster, *History of the Bodleian Library 1845–1945* (1952), pp. 341, 343
125. OM 27.7.1943; A.H.T. Robb-Smith, *A Short History of the Radcliffe Infirmary* (1970), pp. 117–18
126. *Wychwoods History* 8 (1993), pp. 8, 14
127. *COHS Magazine* 4 (April 1943), p. 19
128. OM 31.1.1941
129. Craster, op. cit., p. 343
130. Lennard Bickel, *Rise Up to Life* (1972), pp. 122–4; Gwyn Macfarlane, *Howard Florey: The Making of a Great Scientist* (1979), pp. 328–33; Robb-Smith, op. cit., pp. 178–80; COS OHA Tape 138
131. *Dorn Valley*, pp. 60–1

Chapter Seven
1. BanA 3.10.1940, 10.10.1940
2. Ibid. 13.3.1940, 5.6.1940; William Potts, *History of Banbury* (2nd edn, 1978), p. 327
3. OCA Mayor of Oxford's Scrapbook 1939/40, p. 170
4. Burford and Fulbrook WI, *Burford in the War of 1939–1945* (1947), p. 51
5. OM 29.3.1941
6. COS *Safety First* (July 1940)
7. OM 12.7.1940
8. OCA S261|1|A1|4
9. OCA Mayor of Oxford's Scrapbook 1939/40, pp. 239, 301; 1940/1, p. 10
10. BanA 4.9.1940; CNA 5.12.1940
11. FA 30.8.1940
12. Ibid. 13.9.1940, 29.11.1940
13. OCA Mayor of Oxford's Scrapbook 1939/40, p. 246; ibid., 1940/1, pp. 17, 19, 26
14. CNA 25.9.1940
15. OM 12.9.1941
16. BicA 12.11.1943
17. CNA 11.12.1941; HS 30.6.1944
18. *It Happened in the Dorn Valley* (1946), p. 41; Burford and Fulbrook WI, op. cit., p. 52; OM 10.5.1945
19. OM 10.5.1945
20. CNA 8.7.1943
21. Burford and Fulbrook WI, op. cit., p. 59
22. COS G. Fray, ed., *Current Events and Wartime Benson* (1946), p. 98
23. COS *Safety First* (June 1941)
24. CNA 21.11.1940
25. OA Thame UDC Min. Book 1942/3
26. HS 7.1.1944, 18.2.1944
27. OCA Mayor of Oxford's Scrapbook 1940/1, p. 292
28. *Wootton: A Record of the War, 1939–1945* (1946), p. 4; Charlbury WI, *Charlbury War Record* (1946), p. 25
29. BicA 25.2.1944
30. OCA Mayor of Oxford's Scrapbook 1939/40, p. 357
31. COS *Oxford Monthly* (Feb, Apr 1940)
32. BanA 17.4.1940
33. BicA 15.3.1940; CNA 11.4.1940
34. NBH 27.10.1939; OA Thame UDC Min. Book 1939/40
35. OCA Mayor of Oxford's Scrapbook 1939/40, p. 241
36. NBH 20.11.1939
37. *Dorn Valley*, p. 53
38. Burford and Fulbrook WI, op. cit., pp. 21–2
39. BanA 27.3.1940
40. CNA 5.3.1942; OA Henley BC Min. Book 1941/2, p. 274
41. Ibid. 11.6.1942
42. OA Thame UDC Min. Book 1942/3
43. OM 20.12.1942
44. COS WLWO Museum 15
45. OT 16.4.1943
46. CNA 18.7.1940
47. Charlbury WI, op. cit., p. 14; TG 20.8.1940; OM 5.8.1940
48. OCA Mayor of Oxford's Scrapbook 1939/40, p. 213; OM 5.7.1940

49. OM 12.8.1940
50. OCA S261|1|A1|4; OCA Mayor of Oxford's Scrapbook 1939/40, p. 324
51. NBH 2.8.1940
52. Ibid. 26.7..1940; OM 2.8.1940; COS Fray, op. cit., pp. 130–1
53. OCA Mayor of Oxford's Scrapbook 1940/1, p. 254
54. CNA 20.11.1941
55. Ibid. 27.11.1941; OM 4.4.1942
56. OCA Special Committees Min. Book 1941/2, p. 217; *Eynsham Record* 7 (1990), p. 34
57. OA Thame UDC Min. Book 1942/3; OA T/SL 58(ii)
58. OA Area responses to Government salvage circular, 22.4.1940; OCA Mayor of Oxford's Scrapbook 1939/40, p. 58
59. OM 12.5.1942
60. BicA 4.8.1943; OM 2.1.1942
61. OM 21.10.1942
62. CNA 16.1.1941
63. HS 25.8.1944
64. COS WLWO 16

Chapter Eight
1. OM 29.8.1939
2. OCA Mayor of Oxford's Scrapbook 1939/40, p. 225; R.A. Cooke, *Track layout diagrams . . .* Section 27 (1987), pp. 15, 24
3. WG 10.11.1939
4. OM 1.11.1939, 28.11.1939, 6.1.1940
5. CNA 11.1.1940; OM 8.1.1940
6. FA 19.1 1940
7. Burford and Fulbrook WI, *Burford in the War of 1939–1945* (1947), pp. 54–5
8. E.J. Lainchbury, *Kingham: The Beloved Place* (1957), p. 238
9. Ibid.; Susan Briggs, *Keep Smiling Through* (1975), p. 155
10. OA CCC 1121
11. OA Baldons Produce Guild papers
12. TG 22.10.1940
13. CNA 12.6.1940
14. OM 24.2.1943
15. Burford and Fulbrook WI, op. cit., p. 55
16. BanA 17.7.1940
17. Bodl MS Top Oxon e 289, p. 91
18. OM 19.11.1940
19. CNA 15.5.1941
20. Burford and Fulbrook WI, op. cit., p. 26
21. OA Thame UDC Min. Book 1941/2
22. BicA 1.3.1940
23. *Oxford Monthly* (Aug 1940)
24. COS *Safety First* (March 1942)
25. COS WLWO 26
26. OM 3.10.1941, 27.7.1944
27. Briggs, op. cit., p. 161

28. S.P.B. Mais, *Buffets and Rewards* (1952), pp. 89–90
29. COS WLWO Home Life 11
30. OM 21.5.1943; OCA City Engineer's Dept Newscuttings, 1939–42, p. 87
31. OM 16.6.1943
32. Josep Trueta, *Surgeon in War and Peace* (1980), p. 145
33. COS *Safety First* (Mar 1942)
34. Burford and Fulbrook WI, op. cit., p. 26; CNA 13.10.1939; supra, . . .
35. Humphrey Carpenter, *J.R.R. Tolkien* (1977), p. 193; Trueta, op. cit., p. 146
36. COS WLWO 3
37. NBH 21.6.1940
38. COS *Oxford Siren* (July 1940)
39. BanA 21.2.1940
40. Burford and Fulbrook WI, op. cit., p. 24; Briggs, op. cit., p. 150
41. COS G. Fray, ed., *Current Events and Wartime Benson* (1946), p. 285
42. COS WLWO 3
43. COS WLWO Home Life 11
44. NBH 4.6.1940; *Oxford Medical School Gazette* 41, 1 (1990), pp. 9–10
45. OA CCC 1107(i)
46. OM 6.1.1941; OCA Mayor of Oxford's Scrapbook 1940/1, p. 49
47. OM 29.4.1941; OCA Mayor of Oxford's Scrapbook 1940/1, p. 339; Oxford City Council Reports 1942/3, p. 534; ibid., 1944, p. 420
48. OA CCC 1107(i)
49. CNA 7.1.1943
50. OA CCC 1107(i)
51. Burford and Fulbrook WI, op. cit., p. 24
52. OA CCC 1107(ii)
53. *Wootton: A Record of the War 1939–1945* (1946), p. 3
54. OA CCC 1107(i)
55. Oxon MOH Report 1944, pp. 5–6
56. OA CCC 1107(ii)
57. OA Kirtlington P.C.V.6
58. COS Fray, op. cit., p. 285
59. BicA 16.2.1940
60. OA B7/X/9
61. OM 21.10.1940
62. Briggs, op. cit., p. 217
63. OM 17.3.1942
64. Alan Jenkins, *The Forties* (1977), p. 91
65. OM 7.4.1943
66. HS 28.1.1944
67. Burford and Fulbrook WI, op. cit., p. 26
68. COS WLWO 3
69. OM 3.3.1944, 15.3.1944, 14.9.1944, 21.12.1944
70. Jenkins, op. cit., p. 91; Burford and Fulbrook WI, op. cit., p. 26; COS OHA VT 54

71. OM 19.7.1943; WLWO 29
72. OM 25.11.1943, 10.5.1945
73. Malcolm Graham and Melanie Williams, *When the Lights Went Out: Oxfordshire, 1939–1945* (1979), p. 30
74. COS WLWO Home Life 11; WLWO Banbury Museum receipt
75. CNA 20.3.1941
76. BanA 18.11.1942
77. OM 9.12.1944; W.K. Hancock, *British War Economy* (1949), p. 173
78. OM 2.7.1940; Muriel Groves, *Records of Milton and Shipton-under-Wychwood during the War* (1948), p. 6
79. BicA 27.10.1939
80. OM 15.8.1940, 6.12.1940
81. Oxford City Council Reports 1941/2, pp. 202–5
82. OCA Holidays at Home folder 1943
83. COS Oxford City Byelaws 57
84. Graham and Williams, op. cit., p. 31
85. CNA 28.10.1943
86. COS WLWO M16; WG 8.9.1939
87. OM 15.2.1943, 10.1.1944, 9.2.1944, 14.9.1944
88. Paul Karau, *The Henley-on-Thames Branch* (1982), p. 49; S.C. Jenkins, *The Fairford Branch* (1985), pp. 46, 67
89. *American Oxonian* (April 1941), pp. 81, 83
90. Hancock, op. cit., p. 482
91. OM 6.3.1944
92. E.R. Lawton and M.W. Sackett, *Bicester Military Railway* (1992), p. 62
93. OM 27.5.1944
94. supra, p. 50
95. S.C. Jenkins, op. cit., pp. 68–9
96. American Oxonian (April 1941), p. 83
97. Briggs, op. cit., p. 112
98. COS WLWO 45
99. Briggs, op. cit., p. 112; Alan Jenkins, op. cit., p. 137
100. OM 8.1.1943
101. BicA 29.10.1943
102. CNA 1.2.1940
103. Hancock, op. cit., p. 493
104. Burford and Fulbrook WI, op. cit., p. 26; CNA 31.7.1941; Briggs, op. cit., p. 113; Groves, op. cit., p. 28
105. Wootton, p. 3
106. OM 5.3.1942
107. OA CCC 1121
108. COS Park Hospital Annual Report (1943), p. 4
109. OM 2.9.1939
110. COS Fray, op. cit., p .206
111. Alan Jenkins, op. cit., pp. 73–81; Briggs, op. cit., p. 200

112. OM 18.3.1941, 11.8.1941, 7.1.1944
113. W.R. Nicholson, Here and There (1974), p. 8;
114. OM15.1.1944, 24.9.1944
115. BanA 15.9.1939; CNA 3.11.1939
116. OM 9.8.1940
117. BicA 19.11.1943
118. COS New Theatre programmes
119. COS *Oxford Playhouse 1938–1959* (1959), p. 5
120. OM 8.8.1940
121. OM 2.8.1940
122. OCA Holidays at Home folder 1943
123. BanA 23.7.1943
124. Burford and Fulbrook WI, op. cit., p. 56
125. *It Happened in the Dorn Valley* (1946), p. 57
126. COS Fray, op. cit., p. 284
127. BanA 24.7.1940
128. COS Fray, op. cit., p. 232
129. *Evacuees and Bicester* (1977), p. 28
130. BanA 13.11.1940
131. COS Lloyd papers
132. *Wootton*, p. 2; OM 12.5.1944
133. TG 16.1.1940
134. OM 31.10.1939; BanA 19.10.1939
135. FA 20.9.1940; HS 4.2.1944, 29.9.1944
136. OM 23.3.1944
137. COS OHA OT83
138. OM 16.5.1944; Oxford City Council MOH Report 1944, p. 33; ibid., 1945, p. 42
139. Graham and Williams, op. cit., p. 33

Chapter Nine

1. *It Happened in the Dorn Valley* (1946), p. 70
2. Ibid., p. 70–1
3. Burford and Fulbrook WI, *Burford in the War of 1939–1945* (1947), p. 27–8
4. COS WLWO VE Day notes
5. E.J. Lainchbury, *Kingham: The Beloved Place* (1957), p. 260; OM 10.5.1945
6. BicA 11.5.1945
7. COS WLWO 95
8. OM 8.5.1945, 10.5.1945
9. *Elle* (November 1992)
10. Oxford City Council Reports 1944/5
11. OM 10.5.1945
12. COS Howse papers 1945
13. CNA 10.5.1945
14. BicA 24.8.1945
15. CNA 16.8.1945
16. COS G. Fray, ed., *Current Events and Wartime Benson* (1946), p. 101
17. Lainchbury, op. cit., p. 260
18. BicA 17.8.1945, 24.8.1945
19. OA CCC 1241

@t1a:Index

Index

Page numbers in italic type refer to illustrations